on track ...

The Divine Comedy

every album, every song

Alan Draper

SONICBOND

sonicbondpublishing.com

Sonicbond Publishing Limited
www.sonicbondpublishing.co.uk
Email: info@sonicbondpublishing.co.uk

First Published in the United Kingdom 2024
First Published in the United States 2024

British Library Cataloguing in Publication Data:
A Catalogue record for this book is available from the British Library

ISBN 978-1-78952-308-9

Typeset in ITC Garamond Std & ITC Avant Garde Gothic
Printed and bound in England

Graphic design and typesetting: Full Moon Media

Follow us on social media:
Twitter: https://twitter.com/SonicbondP
Instagram: www.instagram.com/sonicbondpublishing_/
Facebook: www.facebook.com/SonicbondPublishing/

Linktree QR code:

Acknowledgements

First off, my heartfelt thanks go to Stephen Lambe and all at Sonicbond Publishing for the opportunity to get this labour of love published. Also, I would like to say a special thank you to my dear friend and musical colleague, Tim Scott, for introducing me to the music of The Divine Comedy all those years ago. Love and thanks always to my brother Bruce, sister Diane Perry and her husband Nick and to my beautiful wife Radiance, who, as ever, gave me endless moral support, encouragement and love, as well as helping with the photography.

In researching the timeline of The Divine Comedy, I made extensive use of the wonderful online resource *A Short Site About The Divine Comedy* (*ashortsite.com*), which contains a mine of information about all aspects of Neil Hannon's considerable musical output – any DC fan could lose themselves for hours perusing facts and figures about all things DC on this site. Also useful were the superb transcriptions and scores of both Charlotte Gres and Richard Holland – these proved invaluable to me in aiding my overview of those tracks with orchestral arrangements. The website *genius.com* was another useful touchstone for my research, as well as the official Divine Comedy website (*thedivinecomedy.com*) and The Official Charts website (*officialcharts.com*).

Finally, I would like to dedicate this book to Neil Hannon, whose music has enriched my life immeasurably and continues to do so. Many thanks, Neil!

on track ...

The Divine Comedy

Contents

Introduction

In the early 1980s, Northern Ireland was always somewhat neglected when it came to the schedules of major UK touring bands, mainly due to reverberations from 'The Troubles', which had caused huge upheavals in the Province during the 1970s and 1980s. However, this didn't inhibit many aspiring local musicians from forming their own musical combos. In 1984, one of these hopefuls was 14-year-old Neil Hannon, the son of a clergyman: the Rev. Brian Hannon, Bishop of Enniskillen. Neil Hannon purchased his first guitar for £25 from school friend Laurence Hoy, a fellow pupil at Enniskillen's Portora Royal School, an institution famous for having nurtured several notable pupils, including writers Oscar Wilde and Samuel Beckett.

At this time, Hannon was already experimenting at home with two tape recorders, using old suitcases for drums. He also sang in the church choir and his choral experience led to him being selected to perform 'Pie Jesu' in a short movie produced for the opening of Marble Arch caves near Enniskillen in May 1985. By this time, Hannon was also performing in jamming bands with schoolmates, including Laurence Hoy, Ivor Talbot and drummer Maurice Dickson. Most of his school crowd preferred heavy metal, but Neil favoured the pop of ELO, who would prove to be an enduring influence on his musical development through the years.

His first 'serious' band convened in 1986 when, along with Laurence Hoy on guitar and David Graham on bass, he formed the band October. They rehearsed at Hannon's home, The Rectory, and managed to procure a few local gigs in Enniskillen, including a date at the Technical College, supporting The Muck Spreaders. Most importantly of all, he had begun writing songs for the band to perform. These formative attempts at songwriting included the songs 'Passion Fruit' and 'Lady In Lace'. Echoes from these earlier compositions would eventually be heard in his later, more celebrated work. Before 1986 had drawn to a close, October had been furnished with a Boss DR220 drum machine, purchased on a trip to Belfast in November that year and generously funded to the tune of £110 by Hannon's father (who was now the Bishop of Clogher, located in Fivemiletown, just outside Enniskillen). By the close of 1986, keyboardist Darren Flanagan had joined October, filling out their live sound.

Towards the tail-end of 1987, October felt ready to record their first demo tape and headed for Splash Studios in Belfast, where the four-piece line-up of Hannon, Hoy, Graham and Flanagan recorded four Neil Hannon songs: 'Nobody Wins', 'Passion Fruit', 'Silent Man' and 'October', accompanied by the Boss DR220 drum machine. The new tape was dubbed *October 1st* and was recorded for a total cost of £125.

On 8 November 1987, an IRA bomb exploded in Enniskillen, causing a huge amount of death and injury and devastating the town. This had a profound effect on the young Hannon, who penned the song 'Remembrance Day' and would reflect again on this tragedy a decade later in 'Sunrise', the closing track from one of his finest albums: *Fin De Siecle*.

Throughout the next year, October began to shrink, firstly, with the defection of Darren Flanagan in December 1987, followed by David Graham in August 1988 – both left the band to start at University. This left the duo of Neil Hannon and Laurence Hoy, who returned to Splash Studios in January 1989 to record the tape album *Exposition*. This contained ten new Hannon songs: 'Ridgeway Street', 'Suffer In Silence', 'Burdy', 'Wake Up', 'Remembrance Day', 'Dead Or Alive', 'Sands Of Time', 'I'll Be There (With A Gun In My Hand)', 'Roselyn' and 'Stream Of Unconsciousness'.

On 24 June that year, Hannon attended a gig by REM in Dublin, a band that would initially prove to be a major influence on his writing and performing style. As October changed their name to The Cherry Orchard (influenced by the Anton Chekhov play), his brother Brendan introduced him to drummer Kevin Traynor and bassist John McCullagh. Along with this new rhythm section, he and Laurence Hoy headed into Active Studios in Banbridge, County Down, to record a demo that would form the basis of the first album by The Divine Comedy (as The Cherry Orchard were renamed in late 1989). It was at this juncture that Laurence Hoy left the band and The Divine Comedy went forward as a three-piece, with manager Gary McGrade now looking after their affairs.

The final piece of the jigsaw fell into place when McGrade's efforts for the band were rewarded after Rough Trade sent a copy of the demo to indie label Setanta Records. Hannon subsequently signed with Setanta in November 1989, thus starting a chain of events that would lead to The Divine Comedy becoming Setanta's most successful chart act over the next ten years.

Fanfare For The Comic Muse (1990)

Personnel:
Neil Hannon: vocals, guitar
John McCullagh: bass, backing vocals
Kevin Traynor: drums, percussion
Recorded at Homestead Studios, Randalstown, Belfast in May 1990
Engineer: Lorcan MacLoughlann
Producer: Sean O' Neill
Mixed by Mudd Wallace
Record label: Setanta
Released: 30 July 1990
Highest UK chart position: did not chart

Once Neil Hannon had signed the deal with Setanta Records, the label took full control over the management of The Divine Comedy from Gary McGrade. The three-piece line-up entered Homestead Studios in Randalstown, Belfast, in April 1990, with former Undertones guitarist John O'Neill producing (his name spelt the Irish way, as Sean O'Neill on the album credits). Although nominally the producer, O'Neill bowed to Hannon's production ideas during the recording sessions, showing that even at this early stage in his recording career, Hannon knew what he wanted for his songs.

Seen in the context of the complete canon of The Divine Comedy's output, *Fanfare* comes across as a formative album. The next release, in 1993, would see a quantum leap in terms of the maturation of Hannon's still developing muse, with a similar differential to the qualitative leap between Genesis' debut album *From Genesis To Revelation* and their second effort *Trespass* – to give an example from a few decades earlier. The music on *Fanfare* was firmly under the spell of REM, resulting in a minimal-sounding set of songs that was dubbed 'jangle-rock' at the time. There were still some small clues as to where Hannon's lyrical and musical talents might eventually lead, even though originality proved to be a bit thin on the ground on this debut release.

The album was released on 30 July 1990 and drew several appreciative comments from reviewers: Leo Finlay in *Sounds* compared it to the sound of The Byrds and REM, praising Hannon's songs as 'surprisingly intelligent', while Jerry Smith in *NME* dubbed the album 'wondrously minimal'. In truth, Setanta were still setting up their distribution network, which didn't help sales, and by the time they deleted the album from their catalogue a few years later, it had allegedly sold around 200 copies. It was a release that was later disowned by Hannon and he would thenceforth regard the 1993 release *Liberation* as the first 'proper Divine Comedy album', which is a bit of a shame, really, as *Fanfare* is certainly not without merit.

Meanwhile, in April 1990, the band relocated from Northern Ireland to Tottenham in North London, moving in together and using this as a base to promote their debut album with a series of low-level gigs. In August 1990, the band recorded the EP *Timewatch*, which Setanta would hold back until November 1991, by which time, Hannon had inducted long-time mate John Allen into the band on vocals, after losing confidence in his own singing. This new line-up recorded another EP, *Europop*, at Elephant Studios, London, with Edwyn Collins producing, and this was released by Setanta on 10 February 1992. By April of that year, both Kevin Traynor and John McCullagh decided to return to Ireland to continue their studies, calling an end to the formative line-up of the band. Going forward, John Allen became Neil Hannon's personal assistant and it was left to Hannon to re-invent The Divine Comedy, which he would do in spectacular fashion a few years later.

'Ignorance Is Bliss' (Hannon)

With jangly arpeggio guitar chords that sound a dead ringer for Hannon's concurrent musical heroes REM, *Fanfare* opens with a Hannon lyric that first supports, then opposes, the motion that 'Ignorance is bliss', amusingly rhyming this in the chorus with the phrase, 'Whoops, Apocalypse!'. The guitar on this track and, indeed, on most of the album, is basically deployed using two different styles: picked arpeggios and a variety of chord-thrashing techniques, with only the occasional attempt at lead lines. The tempo is mid-paced, and in the verses, there is an attractive spread of vocal harmonies featured that are well-arranged and give the track character.

'Indian Rain' (Hannon)

Moving into triple-time for the second track, there is a U2 influence at play here (another band Hannon witnessed live in Dublin a few years earlier). The verses are mainly worked around one minor chord, with small variations, and the song has a relentless sway to it, falling back to just drums, bass and vocal for the second verse. It then ramps up to be driven along with high energy, including an intense, scrubbed rhythm guitar solo high up on the neck of the guitar that sounds like a demented banjo player on steroids! The lyrics appear to strive for some kind of personal rebirth and evince a cathartic feel.

'Bleak Landscape' (Hannon)

After the intensity of the previous track, we are back to guitar arpeggios on this almost folk-flavoured melody that exudes a laid-back charm and provides the high point of side one. With an engaging tune, this is one of the tracks on this debut that hints at what Hannon would later achieve once he had found his true muse. The verse plays around with a simple major to suspended chord scheme that allows the melody to breathe nicely. This eventually leads to a chorus that resolves the searching lyrics with the notion of escaping across a 'bleak landscape'.

'Tailspin' (Hannon)
A burst of guitar feedback leads into this punk-like thrash with ranted lyrics – it sounds like it could have been minted a decade earlier. Lyrically, it is vaguely political with echoes of Hannon's green agenda, which would crop up again later in the album. Although carried along with power and passion, it is too derivative to add up to much. The track ends in a welter of feedback and guitar-thrashing, closing side one in an extremely noisy manner.

'The Rise And Fall' (Hannon)
Side two opens with a track recalling the feel of 1960s American folk-rock a la The Byrds, albeit through the more contemporary filter of the ever-dominating REM influence. However, such inspiration seems to override most of Hannon's more original musical instincts, which find little space for expression as *Fanfare* unfolds. A typically intense love song, 'The Rise And Fall' features more guitar arpeggios morphing into rhythmic chord work. On the picked passages, there appears to be an extra overdubbed guitar played through some sort of pedal that makes it sound almost keyboard-like. The minor key verses move into a chorus that sports a tumbling melody with a memorable lilt, although the unrelenting minor chords evince a somewhat downbeat atmosphere.

'Logic vs Emotion' (Hannon)
A green agenda returns for one of the album's best songs, again giving the merest hint of what's to come from Hannon once he gets a musical grip on what he really wants to do. More expansive than anything else on *Fanfare*, this track marries a well-crafted lyric to an appealing chord scheme, the verse showcasing some interesting variations around a major chord before arriving at a distinctive chorus. It features a lyric that sees an old lady beseeching the powers that be to 'Leave my house alone', and the woodland creatures metaphorically join in on the chorus with, 'Leave our valley alone'. The short-term folly of humankind is contrasted with the longer timescales of the natural world, which was here before us and will outlast us, no doubt.

'Secret Garden' (Hannon)
A love song with a lusty thrust, couched in poetic metaphor, 'Secret Garden' closes the album with yet more REM influence displayed in the music, which features arpeggio guitar moving over minor chords. This eventually builds into a more thrashed, noisy climax, in which the manic guitar and feedback melt together into an almost psychedelic melange. It has to be said that *Fanfare* is an album that is a touch derivative, but at least Neil Hannon now had a foot in the door and his progress from this point onward would be exponential. He would very soon go on to far greater achievements and chart success.

Liberation (1993)

Personnel:
Neil Hannon: vocals, guitars, keyboards, arrangements, all other instruments apart from those listed below
Darren Allison: drums, percussion
Lucy Castle: viola, violin
Monica Scott: cello
Quentin Hutchinson: French horn
Recorded at Fundamental Studios, Crouch End, London in March 1993
Mixed at The Lab and The Drugstore, London
Engineer: Darren Allison
Producer: Neil Hannon
Record label: Setanta
Released: 16 August 1993
Highest UK chart position: did not chart

Following the demise of the three-piece line-up in April 1992, Neil Hannon returned home to Northern Ireland, there to lock himself away in his room while he composed the material that would constitute his next two albums: *Liberation* and *Promenade*. His latent talent seemed to suddenly switch on and he created the blueprint for his first two true masterworks in a creative frenzy that beggared belief. Ensconced in his parents' attic, he then employed a four-track tape recorder to demo his next album *Liberation*. By March 1993, Hannon felt ready to record the album and Setanta booked him into Fundamental Studios in Crouch End, London, for four weeks. The results proved to be spectacular: the breadth of The Divine Comedy's new sound palette suddenly expanded Hannon's songs from grainy black and white into widescreen colour.

The photoshoot for the album cover took place at Richmond Park, London on 3 May. Photographer Kevin Westenburg snapped Neil Hannon, who, sporting freshly shorn hair (dyed a dazzling yellow!), was dressed smartly in a suit and a tie and wearing shades. This head and shoulders image of him holding onto a park gate was set against the backdrop of one of London's most attractive open spaces. On the final cover shot, both the sky and Hannon were tinted a yellowish hue, contrasting with the green fields in the background.

The album was released on 16 August, and Hannon performed some promotional gigs, accompanied by Chris Worsey on cello and Natalie Box on violin, including a support slot with Blur at Kentish Town Forum on 7 October. In most instances, the press responded favourably to *Liberation*: Ian Cranna in *Q Magazine* commented on Hannon, 'It's sometimes difficult to tell if he's being serious or not', Stuart Clark in *Hot Press* opined, 'If this LP only sells half-a-dozen copies, it'll still be a triumph' and *Select* were of the opinion that *Liberation* was 'One of the most bountiful, overflowing joys of the year – any year'.

A voracious reader, Hannon openly admitted to 'Using novels as a shortcut to wisdom'. One book, in particular, influenced his first tranche of Divine Comedy albums: *A Room With A View* by EM Forster proved to be a revelation to him, and he subsequently devoured all of Forster's novels. A quote from Hannon best sums up *Liberation*: 'I threw off the shackles of indie-pop and was able to write music. It was *Liberation* by name and nature'.

'Festive Road' (Hannon)
After a smidgen of birdsong, the first sounds to greet our ears on this opening track are eight bars of gloriously cascading, tinkling piano notes. Each bar consists of a triplet followed by two pairs of quavers, tumbling ever downwards, akin to a stream burbling over rocks. This leads us into the first verse of a short song in praise of the 1970s TV show *Mr. Benn*. The titular character of this programme would leave his home at 52 Festive Road and enter a costumiers' shop, there to swap his suit and bowler hat for all sorts of exotic costumes. Once he stepped through a magic portal, it would then lead him into a world of adventure and discovery, suited to the particular costume he had donned that day. In the spirit of *Mr. Benn*, 'Festive Road' acts as a kind of portal into the world of *Liberation* created by Neil Hannon. The themes featured throughout the album often explore notions of freedom in various guises and 'Festive Road' itself celebrates the freedom to be who you wish to be. This makes a perfect start to our journey of lyrical and musical discovery, as we explore the twists and turns of the eclectic creations featured on this second album by The Divine Comedy.

'Death Of A Supernaturalist' (Hannon)
Strident violin and cello strokes introduce us to the second track, as Hannon explores his next notion of freedom: to throw off the shackles of institutionally imposed mental rigidity and superstition and, instead, embrace the liberty of unfettered self-expression. This reflected the journey of self-discovery he had been on over the previous three years. The violin and cello both swirl with an ornate virtuosity as 1990s chamber-pop is born, marking the start of what has been termed The Divine Comedy's 'baroque years'. The second verse, in particular, recalls Antonio Vivaldi, with its furious semiquaver string attack sawing away under Hannon's lyric. The spoken samples at the start of the song are taken from the Merchant Ivory production of the 1985 film adaption of EM Forster's *A Room With A View*. 'Supernaturalist' proved to be the first of several tracks on *Liberation* that evoke a chilly autumn landscape (and mention that season in the lyric). There is, indeed, an autumnal feel to the music itself, reflected in the minor key verses, with their emotive rising repeated melody. This contrasts with the 16-bar middle section that reverts to a major tonality and lightens the intensity wrought by the minor-key verses, to which we return again as the song points to its conclusion.

'Bernice Bobs Her Hair' (Hannon)

Following the moody chamber-pop of the previous track, 'Bernice' bobs in with a breezy pop bravado and a 1960s-style 'Baa-ba-ba-ba-baa' chanting hook that links the verses. Although featuring minor chords a-plenty, this intro/bridge section has a pop catchiness that makes it hard to get out of the head, once heard a few times. Driven at pace by Hannon's guitar picking, the memorable verse melody is strung over a snaking chord sequence and there are some tricky time signature punctuations in the section following the verses.

The lyrics are based on the F. Scott Fitzgerald short story 'Bernice Bobs Her Hair', first published in the *Saturday Evening Post* in 1920. The song pretty much follows the plot of the novel: Bernice is a Native Indian girl who is tricked by her dominating cousin, Marjorie, who, looking down on Bernice as below her own social standing, talks her into bobbing her flowing hair into a flapper-style cut in an attempt to humiliate her socially. Bernice, however, gets sweet revenge in the end, when she hacks off her sleeping cousin's luxurious braids, before heading to the station to catch a train back to her hometown. In the context of the album, this track would appear to represent another aspect of freedom: that of freedom from domination and imposed social constraints.

'I Was Born Yesterday' (Hannon)

Some staccato keyboard strokes provide a segue from the previous track, evincing a strong Kraftwerk influence through the track's chugging, almost mechanistic feel using minor and major ninth chords. Lyrically, it's a song that turns the well-known saying, 'I wasn't born yesterday', on its head and runs with a similar theme to 'Bernice': that of domination – firstly parental, then latterly, by a partner, judging by the spoken prose between the sung verses. The chant of, 'Why should I let you, walk all over me?', towards the close of the song perhaps indicates that the worm has turned and is now demanding freedom from an all-too-familiar situation that many unfortunate individuals find themselves in.

'Your Daddy's Car' (Hannon)

One of the songs on *Liberation* that dates back to the John Allen period, 'Your Daddy's Car' is widely regarded as a DC classic and would have made a fine single release, with its strong pop melody and catchiness quotient. Inspired by a car drive to Fermanagh with friends, the lyrics describe the adventures of two lovers who drive out to the seaside, get drunk on champagne and wrap the car around a tree, barely escaping with their lives (and actually die in the demo version!), after which they don't feel like driving anymore. Seen by some as a comment on the drink/drive problems in Northern Ireland at the time, the melody is bouncy, peppy and catchier than a dose of the flu! It's another tune that is hard to stop mentally humming after a few passes. Driven by Hannon's piano and pizzicato violins – with a rising melodic sequence in the verses climaxing in suspensions, and a great use, again, of diminished chords in the catchy choruses – Hannon draws the listener into the story with this irresistible melody. It would prove to be a song that would run and run (excuse the pun!), remaining a live favourite throughout Hannon's long career.

'Europop' (Hannon)
Another tune dating back to the period when John Allen was on vocals, it was, in fact, the title track of an EP recorded back in 1991. The version on *Liberation*, though, is brand new and reworked. A parody of 1990s European dance music, it kicks in with a drum box dance beat and a stylish electro-pop synthesiser riff that Vince Clarke may well have envied at the time. This riff is employed as a bridge, as well as an intro. As the riff stops dead, Neil Hannon's vocal enters with a deadpan, deep-toned, 'Hello, what would you like to know?', accompanied by a burbling, sequenced synthesiser bass line. There is some careful sonic layering applied in the shape of what sounds like a pair of overdriven guitars, panned out to each side of the stereo picture, helping to drive the beat along. The lyrics reflect on the love of money and call into question those with a predilection for the obsessive acquisition of ever-larger amounts of money for the sake of it. It's a brilliantly arranged track that gradually builds, with church organ chords and a choir over the bubbling electro-pop beat on the coda, preceded by the statement, 'What is there left to say?', to which the deadpan answer is, 'Nothing'.

'Timewatching' (Hannon)
This is one of Hannon's most lugubrious creations, with an obvious lyrical debt to the 1952 Victor Young/Edward Heyman song 'When I Fall In Love', famously recorded by Nat King Cole in 1956. Taken at a deadly slow pace, Hannon's vocals are accompanied by an overdubbed cello quartet arrangement, presumably played by cellist Monica Scott. This cello arrangement proceeds at a crawl and lends the track an added mournfulness and a doom-laden feel. Hannon, amongst the slowly groaning celli, croons a lyric that evokes the ultimate undefeatable foe of all living things: time itself. It's a song that had its roots in the title track of the EP *Timewatch,* recorded in 1990, and would be re-recorded in 1997 with a new arrangement for the fifth Divine Comedy album, *A Short Album About Love*. Hannon muses forlornly on mortality and whether his demise may come tonight, tomorrow night, next week, next month or next year, concluding, 'We've only time to fear'. Although brilliantly composed and performed, it's possibly not the best track for anyone suffering from depression to ponder on for too long!

'The Pop Singer's Fear Of The Pollen Count' (Hannon)
This track, however, is the ultimate antidote to the blues and is the most commercial-sounding offering on *Liberation*. A song in praise of the

summertime, with the proviso that you keep your antihistamine tablets with you, 'The Pop Singer's Fear Of The Pollen Count' is one of Hannon's most amusingly jubilant creations to this point and an obvious single, if ever I heard one. That it wasn't chosen as the single from the album was surprising, but it lost out to the more poetic 'Lucy' at the time. All was corrected six years later when, in 1999, a re-recorded version with added brass was released, resulting in a number 17 UK hit single. To my ears, the original on *Liberation* remains the superior version, although both recordings are excellent.

With the announcement, 'Are you ready?', and a joyous shout of, 'OK, let's do it', this upbeat confection gets feet tapping and hands clapping with an early 1970s-style Glitter Band beat and an energetically strummed acoustic guitar accompaniment. Both verse and chorus are the same simple, but uplifting major three-chord sequence. The verse/chorus is adjoined by a clever rising bridge section underpinned by organ triplets, with backing vocal repeats of the lyrics forming the perfect build back into the catchy chorus. It is likely to get most listeners singing the catchy refrain of, 'I'm in love with the summertime'. There are many lyrical puns to cherish en route, involving pill-popping, sneezing, nose-blowing and, in a bit of conceptual continuity, even a lyrical nod to 'Your Daddy's Car' in the second verse. There is a break towards the end where the instrumentation falls back to mainly bass and drums, with an invitation to 'Clap your hands'. A memorable guitar/vocal riff then builds up to an exuberant last brace of choruses (featuring what sounds like a real sneeze at one point!), before the ensemble hammer out a staccato four-note ending, closing this irresistible dose of summery pop music.

'Queen Of The South' (Hannon)

Not a song about Scottish football, as the title might infer (although Hannon would go on to pen some cracking songs about cricket, more of which later!), but rather, this song is about saying the wrong thing whilst in the first flush of infatuation, hinting at unrequited love. It is essentially built on the simple but effective musical device of a chromatic descent around a minor chord and performed at mid-pace on an organ. This effect evokes the feeling of a perpetually revolving spinning top, underpinning the lyrics in the verses.

There are some subtle chord shifts that threaten to belittle this effect as it progresses, but the relentless, cyclic feel remains prominent throughout the entire song. A repetitive but extremely effective guitar riff plays against this matrix, making for a hypnotic atmosphere. Hannon's vocal sounds desperate and pleading after letting his mouth run away with him, and he begs forgiveness from his partner. After the initial verses, there are some lovely vocal harmonies on a repeated chant of the title and they drift seductively across the sound picture – very lush.

'Victoria Falls' (Hannon)
A song that was probably inspired by an incident in Hannon's youth, when he had feelings for a girl named Victoria Scott, back in Enniskillen. She liked the other boys but shut him out. The lyric appears to be on the subject of mental health: a portrait of a girl who is losing her mind and possibly contemplating suicide. The allusion to madness is reflected in the reply vocals to Hannon's lead voice. These raise the image of someone perhaps hearing voices in their head, questioning each line. 'Virginia creeps through her hair' perhaps invokes writer Virginia Woolf, who also ended up taking her life after suffering mental problems.

Based on a musical matrix of churning acoustic guitars, the repeated reply vocal makes for an effective reflection against the lead vocal melody. A bridge section links the verses together with soothing, overlapping vocals that are quite lovely and gives the impression of someone trying to ease away the irrational fears of the song's female protagonist, ending with an assurance that he 'won't let Victoria fall'. There are lyrical nods back to earlier tracks on the album, such as 'Death Of A Supernaturalist' and 'Queen Of The South', the latter perhaps being tied to the lyrics of 'Victoria Falls' – both were possibly inspired by Hannon's youthful infatuation with Victoria Scott.

'Three Sisters' (Hannon)
With its title taken from the Anton Chekhov play of the same name, 'Three Sisters' is something of a DC classic. Unlike the older sisters in Chekhov's play, these sisters appear to be constantly taunting and teasing their younger brother. The lyric has a touch of taboo sexuality about it, voiced from the perspective of the younger brother, whose hormones are obviously starting to kick in. The sense of autumn chill that we encountered earlier on *Liberation* returns with a vengeance here. The choruses, also serving as an intro and coda, evoke an icily sweeping magnificence in both melody, chords and lyrics, as Hannon sings of a chilly autumn breeze, stripping the leaves from the trees. His voice is an extraordinary instrument and effortlessly adapts to each song style he attempts, here sounding as desolate and tortured as the protagonist of his lyric. The arrangement is clever and original, with many sonic treats to enjoy. Starting with the chorus as a prelude works well and sets the mood before a brief rest. Then a looped two-beat electronic riff makes a startling appearance and carries on through the verse, as overdriven guitars on either side of the stereo picture hammer along rhythmically and a thumping four-to-the-floor drum drives the verses relentlessly forward, building to the periodic release into the sweeping choruses. The music raises a mental image of a bitter east wind blowing over frozen Russian steppes. This feel is accentuated by an unexpected instrumental interlude, where Hannon plays what sounds like a balalaika in a jerky rhythm that suggests the influence of Russian folk music. As this section closes, there is a final quieter restatement of part of the chorus and the lines, 'That autumn chill, is with me still'.

'Europe By Train' (Hannon)

Using a snare drum and clipped cymbal splashes, drummer Darren Allison brings to life the vision of an ever-accelerating train leaving the station for this instrumental journey across Europe. Once the rhythm is up to locomotive cruising speed, this densely toned, rhythmically repetitive instrumental works its way perpetually through a repeated rising sequence that has something of an Eastern European feel for the most part. The tonal texture sounds like many instruments have been combined and the mandolin stands out, giving this track its singular feel. Towards the close, the tempo decelerates, bringing to mind an express arriving at its final destination. Eventually, we come to a dead stop and it's the end of the line.

'Lucy' (Hannon, Wordsworth)

In 1992, Hannon discovered the five so-called 'Lucy' poems by the English poet William Wordsworth. These were not grouped as such by the poet himself, being composed as separate entities during different periods, but they are usually referred to collectively by this term. After due consideration, Hannon put aside the third and fourth poems but noticed that the remaining three suggested a similar rhythm, so he decided to use the sequence of the fifth, second and first poems to set to music. At the demo stage, he fully intended to later rewrite his own words to the same rhythm but realised that he was unlikely to better the original words, so kept the poems intact as the final lyric to 'Lucy'. The 'Lucy' poems are referred to by their first lines in lieu of a title, so the opening poem selected, number five, is known as 'I travelled among unknown men'. This poem expresses Wordsworth's love for England and also his passion for an Englishwoman named Lucy.

The musical intro to 'Lucy' features a strummed guitar, employing suspended chords (reminiscent of the opening sequence of 'Pinball Wizard' by The Who) and a steadily paced jogging drum rhythm. The slower, gorgeously sinuous vocal melody, contrasting with the steadier beat, is something that would become a signature style in notable future Hannon compositions. He sings the first two stanzas of the poem, then repeats the final line of the second stanza ('Love thee more and more'), doing the same with the next two stanzas, the repeated line this time being 'Lucy's eyes surveyed'.

For poem number two ('She dwelt among the untrodden ways'), the drum rhythm drops out, leaving a gentle, pastoral feel enhanced by the sound of cows mooing and sheep baaing. When Hannon had recorded the demo version with his window open, the sheep baaing outside had inadvertently ended up on the recording and he so liked the effect that he repeated it for the album version! It proved to be very effective, too, adding an essential dynamic dip to the final recording. After the first stanza of this quieter section, a keyboard, playing arpeggio semiquavers, enters as the arrangement builds back to the re-entry of the drums for the repeated final line of the second stanza ('Shining in the sky'). At this point in the proceedings, Quentin

Hutchinson performs a French horn solo that feels absolutely right for the track. After his short solo, he continues to add French horn phrases beneath Hannon's vocal as it re-enters the fray.

The final 'Lucy' poem employed is number one ('A slumber did my spirit seal'), which is, in many ways, the most moving of them all and worth quoting in full:

A slumber did my spirit seal;
I had no human fears:
She seemed a thing that could not feel
The touch of earthly years

No motion has she now, no force;
She neither hears nor sees;
Rolled round in Earth's diurnal course,
With rocks, and stones, and trees.

William Wordsworth, *Lyrical Ballads Volume 2*, 1800.

This poem represents the poet attempting to come to terms with his loss and the fact that Lucy is now deceased and beyond earthly concerns. In terms of *Liberation*, 'Lucy' represents the spiritual heart of the album, as this closing poem underlines one final aspect of freedom: that of the inevitable and final liberation from the trials of life itself. As the instrumentation drops out, Hannon sings the final line unaccompanied. Wordsworth never sounded so good!

Promenade (1994)

Personnel:
Neil Hannon: vocals, piano, guitar, bass
Natalie Box: violin
Catherine Browning: violin
Jessamy Boyd: viola
Alan Simpson: viola
Chris Worsey: cello
Joby Talbot: oboe, saxophone, cor anglais
Darren Allison: drums, percussion
Recorded at Elephant Studios, Wapping and The Church, Crouch End, London between October 1993 and January 1994
Mixed at The Church, Crouch End; Matrix, London and The Lab, Liverpool
Engineer: Darren Allison
Producer: Neil Hannon and Darren Allison
Record label: Setanta
Released: 28 March 1994
Highest UK chart position: did not chart

In early October 1993, Neil Hannon returned to The Church in Crouch End, London to record tracks for an EP. These consisted of a pair of cover versions: The Throwing Muses' 'Hate My Way' and Edwyn Collins' 'Untitled Melody'. These were released on 18 October as a picture disc EP – *Indulgence No.1* – along with a remix of the *Liberation* instrumental 'Europe By Train'. This was made available by mail order from Setanta Records and the vinyl featured the peculiarity of one side running at 45rpm and the other at 33 1/3rpm. These EP sessions marked a significant moment for Hannon, as it was his first meeting with musician/composer/arranger Joby Talbot, who would work alongside him throughout the 1990s and beyond.

Recording of the next Divine Comedy album, *Promenade*, was also started at The Church Studio sessions in October, with a break for a tour of France (where The Divine Comedy were becoming very popular) in November. This ended with a photo session for the sleeve artwork in Paris on 3 December, again snapped by Kevin Westenberg (who had previously shot the cover for *Liberation*). The front cover again shows a head and shoulders shot of Hannon, smartly dressed in a black suit and tie, wearing shades and standing in front of The Pyramid, close to The Louvre.

Work on *Promenade* resumed in earnest at Elephant Studios, Wapping in December and continued up until 15 January 1994. Released on 28 March, the album proved to be a further variation on the chamber-pop style introduced on *Liberation*. However, this time, it was even more of a concept work than the previous release, relating the story of a day in the life of a young couple who are portrayed as an archetypal hero and heroine. They embark on a quest for that most elusive of life's goals: the pursuit of happiness. This story takes place on a very specific day, as Hannon projects the action six years into the future, setting his tale on 31 December 1999. *Promenade* proved to be possibly *the* most iconic Divine Comedy album; despite evading the mainstream UK album chart at the time, it did manage a number 29 showing on the UK indie chart. The critical reaction to the album reflected an appreciation of its musical and lyrical brilliance: *Melody Maker* hailed it as 'A stolen masterpiece', while *Q Magazine* opined it was 'One of the most unexpected and individual treasures of the year'. In fact, the word 'masterpiece' was bandied about by numerous reviewers at the time and with some justification, as *Promenade* represented a lovingly crafted piece of work, spanning classical, pop and music hall influences, with cinematic and literary references a-plenty.

'Bath' (Hannon)

The water noises that open this track are, in fact, the sound of waves breaking on a remote beach in Druridge Bay on the Northumberland coast. This is a field recording captured by Darren Allison on 28 December 1993. Hannon then recites poetic lines from the 1708 Isaac Watts hymn ('O God, Our Help In Ages Past') that also featured in the 1963 film *Tom Jones* and further samples from this film are employed on subsequent *Promenade* tracks. The long instrumental introduction is an exercise in minimalism, influenced by composers such as Philip Glass and Michael Nyman. Driven by a string quartet, the repeating slurred quavers of the viola and second violin give this intro a slightly seasick feel, exacerbated by the time signature shifting between 7/4 and 6/4. The result is hypnotic, feeling as if the listener is hanging on the edge of some approaching uncertainty. The arrival of Hannon's vocal, accompanied by a bouncing rhythm, brings more solidity to the track as he introduces the heroine of the story, starting her big day with a refreshing bath. Hannon compares her beauty to the mythological Greek goddess Aphrodite and also invokes the nursery rhyme 'Rub-a-dub-dub' to describe the heroine's immersion amongst the soapsuds. Another strong feature of this ingenious arrangement is Joby Talbot's relentless staccato oboe notes that drive the forward, rhythmic thrust of the song.

'Going Downhill Fast' (Hannon)

After our previous introduction to the female character of this story, 'Going Downhill Fast' introduces the male character. Our hero is heading for a rendezvous with the object of his affections via his trusty bicycle, as he rides down an ever-steepening hill. The music is in a brisk triple time rhythm, in which the violin, viola, oboe and piano are prominent, as Hannon sings of the hero feeling alive and in the moment but barely in control, as his bike careers ever-faster downhill. The description of the 'butterflies' tying knots in his stomach ever more urgently is brilliantly expressed by the lyric, and the music itself appears to career along, taking the listener along with the rider on an exhilarating descent. Evoking an expression of the devil-may-care, derring-do attitude of youth, this track proves to be quite a ride. The song was possibly inspired by and based on a place near Londonderry, known as Downhill, where The Bishop's Road leads down through the hills at an ever-steepening gradient. The final couplet of the lyrics demonstrates the truism that 'The bottom is hard, when compared to the top' – as well as being harder to stay in control, it's also harder if you come off the bike and impact with the ground!

'The Booklovers' (Hannon)

On this most cinematic of albums, the first two tracks, which introduced the main protagonists of the story, act as a sort of prequel. This third track could be said to represent the opening film credits, rolling upwards on our imaginary screen. The track starts with a speech sample from actress Audrey Hepburn, taken from the 1957 film *Funny Face*. Following this, Hannon recites an approximately chronological list of 69 authors that have influenced his writing, moving from the likes of Aphra Behn and Miguel De Cervantes in the 16th century, up to the more recent Roddy Doyle and Salman Rushdie. The authors' names are recited by Hannon over a steadily paced 4/4 tempo, featuring an arrangement for a string quartet of violin, viola and two cellos, along with piano and oboe. He interjects witty spoken asides, performed in exaggeratingly funny voices, relating to the characteristics of each author. These are, for the most part, highly amusing, especially as they are juxtaposed against the more serious-sounding music: it's a track that makes me giggle a lot when I'm listening to it. The tuneful chorus is based on a paraphrase of the eighth stanza of *Ode To Man* by the ancient Roman poet Horace. This stanza acts as the central tenet of our hero and heroine's quest for happiness, as the story of *Promenade* unfolds. The chorus stanza will eventually recur in a spoken form to close the album, via a sample of its use in the 1963 film *Tom Jones*. After the couple have finally reached the end of their quest, it will again be quoted in full, to close the album.

'A Seafood Song' (Hannon)

As the couple proceed with their day, their next destination is a seafood restaurant for a spot of lunch. The track opens with a slow tempo, minor key prelude played by a regular string quartet: two violins, a viola and a cello. Over this mournful-sounding backdrop, Hannon slowly chants the chorus of the nursery rhyme 'When The Boat Comes In'. When combined with the lugubrious, minor-key music, it manages to evince a fair degree of gravitas. However, the mood changes to a more celebratory, up-tempo romp, as the hero of the piece raises his glass in a toast to 'Those in peril on the sea': a tribute to the fearless souls who often risk their own well-being to bring seafood to our plates. The verse is pumped along by staccato cello crotchets, as the rest of the strings, along with an oboe, cascade around this rhythm, and Hannon's stomping piano chords underpin this virtuosic swirl. The choruses celebrate a huge range of seafood, pretty much anything fishy – from oysters to octopi, seaweed to swordfish and skate to scampi – gets a mention along the way. The second verse sees the heroine then stand up to deliver her toast to those brave souls who tirelessly labour for the cause: 'In their tiny boats, off John O' Groats'. The track again returns to a minor key for the coda, which is basically a repeat of the prelude, this time as a postlude, closing this fascinating song of gastronomic celebration.

'Geronimo' (Hannon)

While our intrepid couple are occupied consuming their seafood meal, it starts to rain outside. By the time they head out of the restaurant, the rain has become torrential and, clothing-wise, they are ill-prepared for such an eventuality and both get drenched through. After attempting to shelter from the inclement weather, the hero grabs his heroine around the waist and they make a bolt for sanctuary, presumably to his place. This is where, in front of a roaring fire and after divesting themselves of their wet clothing, they presumably consummate their relationship by making love. However, we leave the action just prior to that point in this brief interlude lasting only 1:53. The lyrical action of the song is accompanied by Hannon on piano, playing rapid arpeggios on the beat, while longer lines played on cello underpin a subtle string quartet arrangement. For the first time on the album, there are also several acoustic guitars involved, one of them a nylon string guitar.

'Don't Look Down' (Hannon)

The rain having cleared up, our couple head off to the fun fair for a rendezvous with a rather large Ferris wheel. In a song inspired by Neil Hannon's fear of heights, our rather reluctant hero faces a similar fear, mumbling, 'Ferris wheels, are no big deal', as he holds his lover's hand for reassurance and the wheel begins to turn. Once the wheel approaches its highest point, it all suddenly starts to go wrong, and everything grinds to a halt as they are suspended high above the ground. In the throes of experiencing a meltdown, our hero starts to have an imaginary conversation with a god he doesn't really believe in and the lyrics debate the existence or non-existence of said deity. Our hero's circular and contradictory argument in his head continues as the wind picks up and gets the Ferris wheel turning again. As a result of this, his hysterical fantasy conjures up a bizarre vision of over-zealous angels flapping their wings and causing a zephyr, rather than the more logical reason behind the breeze: the differential between low and high-pressure areas. As his panic abates and the couple reach solid ground again, he suddenly hears a voice that says, 'Don't look down!'

Musically, this episode has an interesting rhythm, being in 12/8 time. The usual string quartet is in attendance, combining with a cor anglais riff that drives the rhythm of the song and a saxophone is also prominent in the arrangement. Hannon sings over an enthusiastically strummed acoustic guitar and also provides piano chords. The brass riffs give the track the feel of a band marching on the spot, fostering a perception of this track as curiously static, perhaps reflecting the breath-holding of the hero as he copes with his altitudinal panic attack.

'When The Lights Go Out All Over Europe' (Hannon)
The next stop for our intrepid couple is an afternoon visit to the cinema – but to view a French art-house film, rather than a Hollywood blockbuster. A trio of French films are referred to in Hannon's lyric: *Jules And Jim* (1962), *Claire's Knee* (1970) and *Breathless* (1960). The last of these provides the sampled dialogue that follows the first chorus of the song. The chorus lyric underlines Hannon's preference for French movies over the American variety, with the assertion that Doris Day couldn't cheer him up 'the way those French girls always could'.

Hannon's cascading, minor-key piano chords give this song a wave-like forward motion against a pulsing bass, supported by a string quartet arrangement with added vibraphone. Joby Talbot's oboe playing is again prominent and the track exudes a sweeping European feel, with a touch of the epic about it. Hannon's strong, clear singing tones demonstrate the emotive power of his voice as he revels in his love for French cinema. The section using the sampled French dialogue from the film *Breathless* is accompanied by some particularly lyrical oboe lines weaving around it. There is a slight deceleration of tempo before resuming for one final chorus, which sees Hannon extemporise vocally on the melody, bringing the song to an emotional conclusion.

'The Summerhouse' (Hannon)
Having exited from the cinema, the couple decide to revisit the scene of the summerhouse, where they used to enjoy summer holidays together when they were younger. This song provides the listener with a backstory to their relationship, in that they had already known each other for quite a while. For this charming interlude, Hannon employs his best Scott Walker vocal impression and the piano carries the forward thrust of the song at a steady mid-tempo pace. This is rhythmically similar to the piano on The Beatles' 'I Am The Walrus', but this song is less chord-intensive than that track. The string quartet provide sustained backing notes that support the vocal/piano front line and Joby Talbot's poignant cor anglais contribution, combined with the nostalgic lyrics, mark this track out as one of the emotional high points on *Promenade*.

'Neptune's Daughter' (Hannon)
Opening with arpeggio piano semiquavers shifting from major to minor over two bars gives this track an oddly unnatural 'swimming' feel from the off. More akin to a classical art song than a pop tune, this is the most

musically oblique track of this collection. The time signature wanders between 4/4 and 3/4, while it also feels harmonically unstable. Despite the convoluted structure, Hannon builds some impressive melodic lines into this floating matrix. The female chorale, which enters at various points in the arrangement, sounds like a purposeful nod to the disorienting choral parts employed by Gustav Holst for his composition 'Neptune: The Mystic', the final movement from *The Planets' Suite*. The arrangement of 'Neptune's Daughter' also features two violins and two cellos weaving around Hannon's woozy piano, and the many references to water on *Promenade* reach a peak on this waterlogged arrangement.

Lyrically, our couple attend a party, but the heroine leaves before attempting to drown herself in the sea. The unstable musical nature of the track perhaps underlines the possibility that the heroine may be suffering from mental health issues. However, the hero comes to the rescue to save the heroine from her potentially watery grave, afterwards comforting her with his love.

'A Drinking Song' (Hannon)

A loud belch precedes this song in praise of alcoholic refreshment, in which the host raises a toast to the nearly drowned couple, as the New Year's Eve celebrations go into full swing. All sorts of alcoholic beverages are consumed to excess to see out the millennium, accompanied by a chorus urging: 'Raise your glasses high, drink the cellar dry!' The time signature is mainly in a brisk 12/8 (with a slight diversion into 9/8 and 6/8 en route), giving the track a general triple-time feel reminiscent of a typical German drinking song. You can imagine beer-filled steins being banged onto a table in time with the tympani beats that drive this song's rhythm. After a few verses, there is a drunken-sounding rendition that starts with 'There'll Always Be An England', before honourable mentions of Ireland, France, Lichtenstein and Finland ensue. The string quartet and saxophone arrangement add to the boozy, woozy feel of the track, as it wends its way to a drunken-sounding climax, where the protagonists and their guests sing of seeing pink elephants inside their heads, beds and the threads of their pyjama legs!

'Ten Seconds To Midnight' (Hannon)

In this song, Hannon cleverly collapses the whole of human evolution into a metaphorical ten-second countdown (although the track itself is 2:10 in duration). The song also sees our intrepid couple on a balcony, counting down the last ten seconds of the 20th century. Accompanied by just his slow, spaced-out piano chords, Hannon's plaintive vocals move downward from ten, one verse at a time, via some movingly philosophical couplets en route, including the prescient, 'How we made it to nine, I'll never know'. He also quotes both Archimedes and Rene Descartes: 'Along comes number five, Eureka! I'm alive, I think, therefore, I am'. It's a track that primes the listener perfectly for the entry of the album's standout track: 'Tonight We Fly'.

'Tonight We Fly' (Hannon)

Rightly regarded by most fans as the ultimate DC classic, this remarkable song is undoubtedly the emotional high point of *Promenade*, as our hero and heroine take flight together into a new century and their future together. The track enters with a galloping snare drum, soon joined by a string trio of two violins and one viola playing staccato quavers a la Antonio Vivaldi over the galloping snare beat. Neil Hannon tops this charging backing track with one of his most beautifully slow and sinuous melodies – a clear indication of musical genius at work. As our couple metaphorically take flight, the whole of humankind appears to be spread out below them as they soar over the 'rooftops, skylights and slates'. It's a song that I personally find incredibly moving – a magical combination of words and music that really sums up all the sadness and lost opportunity inherent in the human condition. As Hannon movingly intones: 'Looking into all your lives and wondering why, happiness is so hard to find' – it is, for me, one of those moments that fill the eyes with tears.

As we fly along with our couple, Hannon's vocals employ the art of canon, with waves of overlapping melody, as we move over those below us, including the doctor, the soldier, the farmer, the poacher, the preacher, the gambler, the teacher, the writer, the lawyer, the dancer, the voyeur, the builder and the destroyer. All human life is there beneath us, until, eventually, we fly 'Over the hills and far away'. The release back into the verse melody is elating in the extreme and the song reaches its climax (and its point) with a final moving stanza that ponders on the moment we leave this planet forever and whether we'll feel 'disappointed or sad' with our lives. As the music rises to its crescendo, we hear the moving lines: 'If heaven doesn't exist, what will we have missed, this life is the best we've ever had'.

'Tonight We Fly' neatly sums up the entire ethos of *Promenade*: that of living in the moment and *being*, rather than continually pondering an uncertain future, a nostalgic past or some imagined afterlife. Maybe the hero and heroine of the story have discovered, via their quest and their love for each other, that perhaps the sharp point of *now*, the moment itself, is where true happiness may dwell.

'Ode To Man' (Horace)

Promenade ends with a sampled quote taken from the 1963 film *Tom Jones*. It is based on the eighth stanza of *Ode To Man* by the ancient Roman poet Horace, as translated by John Dryden. A paraphrase of this quote had appeared earlier on in the album as the chorus to 'The Booklovers'. It is a quote that underlines the central tenet of the story, enacted through *Promenade*:

Happy the man, and happy he alone,
He who can call today his own,

He who secure within can say,
Tomorrow do thy worst, for I have lived today.

Horace, 'Ode To Man', *Odes*, 13BC.

Casanova (1996)

Personnel:
Neil Hannon: vocals, piano, guitar, bass, Hammond organ, Wurlitzer, whistling, timpani, percussion, arrangements
Joby Talbot: piano, alto saxophone, arrangements ('Theme From Casanova' and 'The Dogs & The Horses'), orchestration and conducting
John Allen: celesta, whistling
Padraic Savage, Laura Samuel, Yuri Kalnitz, Eos Counsell, Alex Postlethwaite, Roberto Borzoni, Colum Petitt, Leonie Curtin, Anna Giddey, Mark Knight, Sylvia Kapp, Jethro Shirley-Smith, Rebecca Hayes, Alison Fletcher, Alice Pratley and Emile Chitikov: violin
Charlotte Glasson, Sancia Norman, Alison Fletcher and Nick Milne: viola
Ruth Goldstein, Chris Worsey, Kathy Brown, Jane Watkins and Jo Richards: cello
Sam Burgess: double bass
Alex McRonald: flute
Adrian Roach: oboe
Jill Morton and Mary Bellamy: clarinet
Clare Daley: bassoon
Charlotte Glanson: tenor and baritone saxophones
Judith Goodman: horn
Robin Smith, Titch Walker, Doug Waterston, David Gosland, Joe Gribble and Gregor Clarke: trumpet
Robin South: flugelhorn
Jane Butterfield and Steven Mathieson: trombone
Stuart Bates: bass trombone
Robin Hayward: tuba
Rob Farrer: timpani
Darren Allison: drums, percussion
Jools Pais: guitar
Grant Gordon: bass, drums
Bryan Mills: bass
Alice Reynolds, Maia Lloyd: giggling
Recorded at Milo, Abbey Road, Moles, Rooster, Maison Rouge and Elephant Studios, London between June 1995 and January 1996
Mixed at The Church, Mayfair and The Greenhouse Studios
Engineer: Darren Allison, assisted by Scott Howland, Paul Mysiak, Robbie Kazandjian, Darren Nash, Tom Gurling, Chris Seard, Gerard Navarro and Gareth Parton
Producer: Darren Allison and Neil Hannon
Record label: Setanta
Released: 29 April 1996
Highest UK chart position: 48

In the wake of the release of *Promenade*, Neil Hannon formed a new live band that included Natalie Box (violin), Catherine Black (cello) and Joby

Talbot (piano), with himself on guitar and vocals. This line-up of The Divine Comedy then commenced a tour of the UK and Europe in support of singer/songwriter Tori Amos, running through April and May 1994. This was followed by a headlining tour of France – an increasingly popular market for The Divine Comedy. Some of the performances from these gigs were released on the EP *Indulgence No.2* in July – these were all live versions of songs from *Promenade*: 'A Drinking Song', 'When The Lights Go Out All Over Europe' and 'Tonight We Fly'.

In September, Hannon visited New York, staying with Andy Chase from the NY band Ivy. During this visit, Hannon started writing songs for the next Divine Comedy album and even began some tentative recording at Andy Chase's studio. He also managed to fit in a gig at Acme Underground, supporting Ivy. The end of 1994 saw a re-jigged live DC line-up, which retained Talbot on piano and called in former Hannon schoolmates Bryan Mills (bass) and Grant Gordon (drums), as well as Stuart Bates (organ). This line-up played further dates in France (minus Grant Gordon on occasion, as some venues didn't allow drums), and on a few special dates, they were accompanied by a string quartet.

A significant event occurred in early 1995 when Hannon was asked to compose music for a new Channel 4 TV show: *Father Ted*. He wrote the music for a cod-Eurovision song, 'My Lovely Horse', to be featured in the *Father Ted* episode 'A Song For Europe'. This commission obviously raised Hannon's profile and some of the songs he wrote for *Father Ted* would end up on *Casanova*. Sessions for this album commenced on Midsummer's Day 1995 at The Garden (Studio 3) and Milo (Studio 1), and a combination of London studios would be employed for recording orchestral overdubs, including Abbey Road (Studio 1). Sessions for the album ran through the remainder of the year and into 1996.

The photoshoot for the album cover took place on a trip to Venice at the start of December 1995. Hannon travelled there with his manager Maya Gabrielle and his usual photographer, Kevin Westenberg. For this album, he took on a different identity, becoming 'the cad', eschewing his usual smart appearance and, this time, looking a bit more of a Jack-the-lad. Clad in a denim jacket, wearing his usual shades and with a cigarette in his mouth, he posed by the side of a Venetian canal. The original plan was for the album to be titled *Don Juan*, with a cover shoot in Seville, Spain, but due to an airport strike in Paris, the party ended up getting a plane to Venice instead, hence the change of album title to *Casanova*. Hannon's cad persona dominates the lyrics, while the music also takes a new direction, being generally more pop/rock oriented under the influence of Jarvis Cocker's band Pulp. He did, however, maintain a strong orchestral element in the mix, marshalling even stronger orchestral forces than those used on previous albums, and this would continue throughout the career of The Divine Comedy.

Casanova was released on 29 April 1996 and showcased some of Hannon's most accessible songs yet, but also some of his least accessible compositions. The more commercially slanted songs gave The Divine Comedy an initial taste of substantial chart success, though, with no less than three UK hit singles taken from the album. *Casanova* itself peaked at number 48 in the UK album chart during a 17-week run. Reviews were generally positive: Martin Aston in *Q Magazine* dubbed it 'Music to appeal across all pop tastes', Jason Cohen in *Rolling Stone* called it 'A cheeky, grandiose masterpiece' and Nick Duerden in *Mojo* reckoned it exuded 'Enough lush beauty to make a dictator weep'.

'Something For The Weekend' (Hannon)
Slipping straight into the album's cad character, the opening track commences with a sleazily voiced 'He-llo!' from Hannon, along with some girlie giggling, courtesy of Alice Reynolds and Maia Lloyd. Dripping with sleaze, our Lothario suggests, 'How about a little kiss, oh, don't be unkind', to further giggling from the girls. Over this opening sequence, there are some chimes, sounding like tubular bells, before the track moves into the tempo previously employed on the DC classic 'Tonight We Fly' – that of the galloping snare drum. This rhythm would prove to be one of Hannon's favourites and would recur again on future tracks. He has stated that the inspiration for this track came from Kate Beckinsale's performance in the 1995 film *Cold Comfort Farm*, adapted from a novel by Stella Gibbons.

The song centres on an enigmatic 'something in the woodshed' – it's a mystery that's never completely solved in the lyric and would, in fact, be referred to again a few DC albums down the line. Whether our rascally rake has another woman hidden in the woodshed is a question that springs to mind, as he continually reassures his companion that 'There's nothing in the woodshed, except maybe some wood'. It's an amusing performance with a distinctly creepy undertow. The pop catchiness of the music is irresistible – one of the potential reasons that this track became a number 14 UK hit single in the summer of 1996.

The arrangement is perfection itself, with a contagious beat, driven by the core of The Divine Comedy's concurrent live unit, Hannon's old pals Bryan Mills on bass and Grant Gordon on drums, along with the main man on guitar, organ and vocals. It's an energetic track, spurred on by occasional enthusiastic chants of 'Whoooo!' by the backing vocalists. The middle eight becomes almost funky and very danceable. It all builds up to a wonderful climax, where, this time, the cad gets his comeuppance on a visit to that curious woodshed, as he is whacked on the head, then gagged and bound. When he awakes, he discovers he has been robbed, with his car and all of his money gone, presumably stolen by his inquisitive former companion, but possibly by whoever was occupying the mysterious woodshed!

'Becoming More Like Alfie' (Hannon)

By the second track on *Casanova*, our protagonist's caddish behaviour plumbs new depths, as the lyric to this – the second hit single from the album (a number 27 UK hit in the autumn of 1996) – sees this incorrigible womaniser beginning to get completely out of control. The track opens with a speech sample of Michael Caine and Millicent Martin, taken from the 1966 film *Alfie*. The verse music sounds very much in the style of that era, with a distinct Burt Bacharach feel to its brass-tinged arrangement, moving around variations on a minor chord. Hannon's own inner conflict about the cad persona he adopts for this album is reflected in various lines in the verse, as he sings of a time when his mind lay 'on higher things' and when callous womanising was reserved 'For other guys, less smart than I', as his intellect struggles with more base instincts.

The song boasts a killer chorus, where the ignoble cad just won't take 'no' for an answer (claiming that 'no' means 'yes') and further invoking the era of *Alfie* with the line: 'Just like glasses come free on the NHS'. After the more level feel of the verses, the chorus music employs an inspired rising chord sequence, giving it an irresistible catchiness and a huge degree of pop thrill. Considering this, it's surprising that this second single from *Casanova* wasn't an even bigger hit. Towards the end of the song, there is also a tidy Hannon guitar solo over the chorus sequence, one of his most succinct. It perfectly lines up the denouement of the song, invoking the title phrase before ending on a sixth chord, completing an edifying slice of perfect pop.

'Middle Class Heroes' (Hannon)

This is a song inspired by Hannon's stay in a bed and breakfast decorated in a kitsch fashion. He imagined it as the abode of a young, middle-class, sex-obsessed couple who end up inadvertently bringing kids into the world and having to face up to this unforeseen turn of events. This newly assumed responsibility evidently didn't stretch as far as noticing their three-year-old swallowing the rows of allergy pills that line their shelves. As a song, it's cleverly done but makes for pretty depressing listening. However, Hannon manages to inject some grim humour into the lyrics, especially in the intro, where he plays a seedy-sounding fortune-teller predicting the dour course of their young lives to come in the near future. There are some amusing lines in his fortune-teller spiel before the song proper gets underway. I particularly like his suggestion: 'Cross my palm with plastic and I'll see what I can do'.

Musically, the song has a relaxed tempo, driven by marimba riffs and a sliding trombone, with the orchestra coasting in the background. It sounds lush, laid-back and positively dripping with decadence, using jazzy ninth and flattened fifth chords to good effect.

'In & Out Of Paris & London' (Hannon)

The above title is the one that appears on the sleeve credits for the album, but it's listed in the *Casanova* booklet as 'In & Out *In* Paris & London'. According to Hannon's management, the latter is the correct title (being a parody of the George Orwell book title *Down And Out In Paris And London*). Since the song concerns our inveterate cad indulging in rampant sexual behaviour in these two cities, the latter title also makes more sense.

Driven by a repeated minor-key riff, its repetitive forward motion displays a minimalist feel that becomes somewhat relentless as the listening experience grows ever more uneasy. An electric guitar bashes out rhythmic chords, propelling the track forwards, which is then joined by piano and marimba accentuating the riff. Hannon's vocals sound feverish and the continual 'in, out' chants towards the end render this track almost pornographic in its literal depiction of the sex act. However, the Hannon humour is never far away, and the 'in, out' episodes are split with several chants of 'shake it all about', evoking the well-known party song: 'The Hokey Cokey'!

'Charge' (Hannon)

Although employing militaristic imagery, this song is the second in a row on *Casanova* that is basically about sexual intercourse. With its euphemistic reference to 'cannons' to the left and right, and chants of 'Bang, bang, bang', it suggests our cad is partaking in a sex orgy.

The music has a kind of mutated Latin-American groove but with a stop-start feel to the rhythm. Marimbas are, again, prominent in the arrangement and the track has a somewhat chaotic feel to it, with Hannon's vocals becoming more raucous as the track progresses. By the coda, he is continually yelling out the word 'Bang!' at the top of his voice with an abrasive rasp. There is also a frankly odd, but amusing interlude, where he parodies both soul singer Barry White (the self-proclaimed 'Walrus of love') and 1980s pop sensation Prince. His Barry White impression is unerringly accurate, employing that husky groan that seemed to make women go weak at the knees back in the 1970s. Meanwhile, he adopts a more falsetto mode for Prince, as the two icons exchange their blathering, stretching the metaphor of the 'sexual battlefield' that permeates this strangely inaccessible song. On the subject of this track, Hannon is said to have made the tongue-in-cheek comment, 'This is about as low as I'll ever get. Savour the moment, folks'.

'Songs Of Love' (Hannon)

Following the full-on overkill of 'Charge', the mood then surprisingly shifts to one of romance, expressed in one of Hannon's most sublime pop creations. Voiced by a character who is the polar opposite of our earlier protagonist – a sensitive and romantic 'poet-in-the-garret' type – he observes the doings of the predatory male hordes with an anthropologist's eye. References to 'Pale, pubescent beasts' hunting herds of female 'prey' are contrasted with the more solitary life of the sensitive loner, writing his 'Songs Of Love' in 'bedrooms above' while the mating action goes on down below.

With its gentle triple time swing, this gorgeous pop tune was an obvious choice for a single and probably would have had a wide public appeal, but was passed over in favour of the three hit tracks from the album that were chosen for single release. The song displays an economical arrangement of strummed acoustic guitar, a keyboard sounding like a spinet and some fetching vocal harmonies – especially on the delightful, repeated middle eight. The Hannon trademark of canon-like, overlapping backing vocals is well in evidence, giving the song a lovely harmonic ambience. The melody had originally been composed as the theme music for the Channel 4 sitcom *Father Ted* and, in this capacity, became one of the most widely heard of his works, once this sitcom was aired. 'Songs Of Love' is a perfect pop song that has subsequently been covered by many other artists, including the likes of comedian and TV presenter Alexander Armstrong and Irish crooner Joe Dolan.

'The Frog Princess' (Hannon)

Opening with a blast of the French national anthem 'La Marseillaise' (a distinction it shares with The Beatles' 'All You Need Is Love'), this is an engaging little pop tune and another UK hit single, reaching number 15 in November 1996. The titular 'Frog Princess' proves to be more than a match for our Casanova, who appears to have had stronger feelings for this particular French fancy. However, she sees right through his facade and treats him the way he had been treating his former conquests – much to his chagrin, judging by some of the bitter lines on display here. Regrets? He's had a few, by the sounds of it! In the second verse, Hannon croons, 'I should have left her well alone' (adding the amusingly throwaway, spoken aside, 'But oh no, not me!'), and by verse three, openly admits his regret at this fairy-tale-gone-wrong, shaking his head that just one kiss 'Could turn my frog into a cow!'.

The song boasts a strong chorus, denying love, but the underlying feeling tells a different tale, with the regretful verses giving our hurt cad's true feelings away. Hannon's marvellously flexible voice brings forth some vocal moments to savour, ranging from humorous interjections, passionate crooning and, on the coda, soulful extemporisations. There is a lovely touch in verse four, where our anti-hero is reflecting on what might have been – check out the way he pronounces the word 'visualise' literally (as 'vis-u-a-lise'), then rolls the letter R in 'Fr-r-rog Princess' – a delicious moment. When he sings of imagining his Frog Princess 'beneath a shining guillotine', the music pauses momentarily for the sound effect of a guillotine descending; this was evidently achieved by using a pair of garden shears!

Musically, the song is mainly driven by Hannon's watery-sounding piano, while a horn plays 'La Marseillaise' on the intro, mid-song in lieu of a solo and on the coda, where Hannon soulfully improvises over the top, using variations on the chorus chant, 'You don't really love me'.

'A Woman Of The World' (Hannon)
Written back in 1994, this song was originally intended for use in the sitcom *Father Ted*. Hannon revamped the song and shoehorned it into the *Casanova* concept, where it snuggles into the running order quite well. It was inspired by one of Hannon's favourite movies, *Breakfast At Tiffany's*, starring Audrey Hepburn. Lyrically, it sounds as if our rascally rake is pining for the ultimate, too-hot-to-handle, unobtainable woman.

Musically, the song is given a swinging, big-band treatment, with lavish doses of Hollywood glamour and a production that sounds as if it has arrived straight off Broadway. The jazzed-up, American 1940s-style arrangement brings to mind an old Busby Berkley production, and when the massed male backing vocalists come in on the second verse, you can imagine them all wearing top hats, white ties and tails while performing a hackneyed dance routine behind Hannon, as he croons fetchingly out front. The choruses sound more intimate as the cad imagines how he would cope with this idealised 'super-woman'. Hannon croons, 'Maybe I'll kill her, just trying to thrill her', adding, 'If she don't kill me first'. It sounds as if he may have bitten off more than he can chew with this particular woman!

'Through A Long And Sleepless Night' (Hannon)
A minimalist bleeping sound opens this claustrophobic-sounding track that was created from the remains of unused song ideas in Neil Hannon's notebook. Mostly built on a nagging, repetitive riff in 7/8 time, it is both lyrically and musically breathless and airless in its relentless forward motion. It's only when it moves into a repeated, soul-influenced 4/4 section, sung in a higher register, that we find any breathing space, before resuming its forward charge. Having experienced insomnia, I can attest to the fact that the word-crammed, unrelenting verses of this creation do evoke the less-than-pleasant experience of prolonged sleeplessness. The vocal sound employed becomes more distorted as the track progresses and Hannon's ranting here sounds on the verge of hysteria. The bleeping that opened the track continues under the cacophony and, indeed, closes proceedings as the pitch of the bleep descends and slows towards the end, sounding like expiry from exhaustion or possibly representing a cardiac arrest after too much vigorous lovemaking! Uneasy listening all the way, Hannon himself referred to this uncompromising track as 'Six minutes of paranoia'.

'Theme From Casanova' (Hannon)
Functioning as incidental music, this largely instrumental piece appears to draw a line under the concept of the album so far. The roots of this theme go back to one of Hannon's earliest attempts at songwriting and recycle some melodic ideas from his 1986 composition 'Passion Fruit'. The track has a gently jogging rhythm, like the amble of an old prospector on his mule, riding off into the sunset. Over the first section of this piece, Joby Talbot

imitates a BBC Radio 4 announcer, giving an amusing 'you have just been listening to' rundown on the *Casanova* credits as if it had been a radio production. After this, the music ambles along amiably, with a horn playing the repeated melody as the strings swell behind. The track acts as a sort of extended 'intermission'. This, in effect, separates the main body of the album from the finality of the closing track. As the 'Theme' comes to an end, we hear sound effects of galloping horses' hooves and barking dogs, cueing up the 'standalone' closing track of the album.

'The Dogs & The Horses' (Hannon)
Very much an odd track on this collection, this final offering is a lushly orchestrated minor-key ballad. It uses the analogy of the four seasons to represent a human lifetime. It is beautifully performed but unremittingly downbeat in its ambience. It's one of those songs, though, that, despite its gloom-laden countenance, is oddly uplifting in its fatalistic acceptance of our time-limited span on this planet. By the last verse, we're contemplating finality, as Hannon sadly reflects on his favoured animal species, lamenting the sadness of 'All the dogs and the horses, you'll have to outlive' to even get to old age. Touchingly, he conjures the oft-experienced death-bed phenomenon of mentally 'seeing' deceased loved ones before passing, in this case, his beloved dogs and horses around the bed. This kind of experience is cited by many as evidential glimpses of an afterlife of some kind, while more sober observers put these visions down to mentally generated images, perhaps evolutionary driven, to ease our final moments of consciousness.

Additional Material
'Birds Of Paradise Farm' (Hannon)
Released on the first DC hit single 'Something For The Weekend', this enchanting song sees Neil Hannon in a nostalgic mood, as he casts his mind back to an early holiday when his parents took him to a place called Paradise Farm. This idyllic setting left a deep impression on the young Hannon, leading to this early example of one of his in-touch-with-nature songs that run like a green seam through his output. Recorded with guitar arpeggios panned to one side of the stereo picture and organ to the other, the song is driven by a light Latin rhythm played on rim shots until the second verse, when a full drum kit takes over. Some lovely flute trills appear in the intro, sounding like the fluttering birds of the title. The young Hannon seems mesmerised by the singing birds of Paradise Farm until, to his dismay, he discovers that what he can hear are caged birds rather than free-flying ones.

In the middle eight, he invokes Leonardo Da Vinci and Saint Francis of Assisi. The former had a deep interest in the mechanics of flight and even designed a 15th-century prototype helicopter; the latter was the 12th-century patron saint of animals, with a particular affinity for birds. Here, Hannon contrasts his young self with 'Renaissance Man' Da Vinci and animal-loving

Saint Francis, coming to the conclusion that 'Neil Hannon of the See House, Fivemiletown doesn't seem quite right, somehow'. Some discreet tubular bell sounds are added to the track at this point. An organ solo follows the middle eight and the final verse returns to the laid-back sound of the first, as the trilling flute returns. It's a fine track that many fans rate as one of the best 'B-sides' in the DC canon.

'Love Is Lighter Than Air' (Merritt)
This engaging pop song was composed by Stephin Merritt of American band The Magnetic Fields, originally appearing on their 1995 album *Get Lost*. Neil Hannon's interpretation was also included on the DC single 'Something For The Weekend'. It is an arrangement that, indeed, sounds lighter-than-air, with picked electric guitar chords and organ as the main backing. Hannon sings in his lower range, his nut-brown voice giving the track a distinctive feel. The track has a summery ambience, that season being mentioned several times in the lyrics. The song advises us to grab hold of love while we can and make the most of our opportunities before they 'float away'. The chorus melody is close to that of Simon & Garfunkel's 'Cecilia' from the multi-platinum *Bridge Over Troubled Water* album of 1970. It's catchy in the extreme and Hannon's vocal moves up an octave towards the close of the song to urge home the lyrics.

'Motorway To Damascus' (Hannon)
With a repeated keyboard motif, possibly sequenced, running throughout the track, this rather mechanical concoction recalls German band Kraftwerk, an obvious influence on many aspects of Neil Hannon's music. Some dissonant keyboard-generated sounds drift in and out halfway through the song, adding to the air of mystery displayed by this odd track. Lyrically, we find another example of Hannon's green sympathies, allied with much biblical imagery, as befits a highway to Damascus. The main thrust of the song dwells on the power of nature and the rise and subsequent fall of civilisations, including our own. It imagines the day: 'When the silhouetted ruins of the cooling towers, are but ivy-clad reminders, of a long-forgotten power'. This song appeared on *A Casanova Companion No.3* with the hit single 'The Frog Princess' and was released on 4 November 1996.

A Short Album About Love (1997)

Personnel:
Neil Hannon: vocals, guitar
Joby Talbot: piano, arrangements
Ivor Talbot: guitar
Stuart 'Pinkie' Bates: Hammond organ
Bryan Mills: bass
Miguel Barradas: drums
Simon Baggs, Lisa Betteridge, Kate Birchall, Krista Juanita Caspersz, Emily Davis, Benjamin Harte, Mary Martin, Timothy Myall, Benjamin Nabarro, Juliet Warden: violin
Yannick Dondelinger, Zoe Lake, Jong On Lau, John Murphy: viola
Betsy Taylor, Robbie Jacobs, Duncan Moulton: cello
Peter Devlin, Philip Dawson: double bass
Max Spiers: oboe
Charlotte Glasson: saxophone, flute
Matthew Gunner: horn
Simon Jones: trumpet
Adam Howard: trumpet, flugelhorn
Jane Butterfield: trombone
Robert Farrer: percussion
Christopher Austin: conductor
Deborah Keyser: administration of Brunel Ensemble
Recorded at Shepherds Bush Empire on Fleetwood Mobile with Ian Dyckhoff and Tim Summerhayes between 19 and 20 October 1996
Engineer: Jon Jacobs, assisted by David Tyler and Andy Scade
Mastering: Metropolis Studios by Ian Cooper
Record label: Setanta
Released: 10 February 1997
Highest UK chart position: 13

Following a UK and European tour supporting Supergrass in early 1996, drummer Grant Gordon broke his arm during a football match and was replaced by Miguel 'Miggy' Barradas, prior to the band embarking on their summer gig schedule. This included some high-profile TV dates to promote the hit single 'Something For The Weekend' – including Channel 4's *TFI Friday* on 31 May, BBC 2's *Top Of The Pops* on 28 June and ITV's *Saturday Live* on 6 July. On 6 September, Neil Hannon revisited New York, and while there, he met up with photographer Kevin Westenberg for a photo session, shot near the Guggenheim Museum, which provided the cover artwork for the next Divine Comedy release: *A Short Album About Love*. The cover shot is a dark blue-tinted, side-on profile of Neil Hannon (looking very Brian Eno-like!) through a rain-soaked car window, while the inside cover is another blue-tinged photo of him inside an NYC taxi, taken from outside of the car and influenced by the front cover artwork of the first *Peter Gabriel* album.

The new album was recorded on 19 and 20 October, during rehearsals and sound checks for a gig at Shepherds Bush Empire in London. It was recorded live, but Hannon did re-record some of the vocals later. Backed up by the orchestral forces of the Brunel Ensemble, the sound created was huge and lush and was very much under the influence of the sweeping, orchestral big ballads of the 1960s, particularly those recorded by Scott Walker and The Walker Brothers.

On the album's release on 10 February 1997, reviews were again generally favourable. Stuart Maconie in *Q Magazine* reckoned that it 'Serves to remind us of Neil Hannon's genius', while *Time Out* praised its 'Heart-stoppingly gorgeous, romantic smoochers' and *Vox* called the album 'A mini-masterpiece'. In truth, most of these songs were left over from Hannon's writing for the *Casanova* project but perhaps didn't quite fit into the concept of that album. The idea of recording them live with an orchestra was a good one, though, and he was rewarded with the best-selling Divine Comedy album yet, as it peaked at number 13 in the UK album charts during an 8-week run. By December of that year, it had gone silver. It also spawned a substantial UK hit single when 'Everybody Knows (Except You)' was released in March 1997 and became a number 14 UK hit.

'In Pursuit Of Happiness' (Hannon)

We're back with one of Hannon's favourite lyrical themes here and one on which he had previously expanded, as it formed the central premise of the *Promenade* album a few years earlier. This song contrasts the ecstasy of being in love with the daily peril faced by many in this dangerous and fragile world. Hannon declaims that, come what may, if he is in close proximity to the object of his romantic desires, he'll 'Never be anything other than happy', despite the death and destruction in the world.

Joby Talbot's orchestral arrangement for this song is expansive, with an epic sweep and some interesting harmonic choices. He later adapted some of these melodies into his theme music for the BBC 2 TV programme *Tomorrow's World*. The intro is driven by the brass section playing widescreen seventh chords with added ninths and sharpened ninths, successfully evoking a feeling of perpetual descent, before dropping back to Hannon's strummed guitar chords as the vocals enter the picture. As he croons powerfully, the arrangement builds up behind the vocal and furious keyboard triplets, later doubled with marimba, providing the song with its forward momentum. With a swinging, jazzy vibe to it, the orchestral arrangement grows bigger and bigger as the song goes along, feeling like epic soundtrack territory in places. For the coda, it falls away to just Hannon's strummed guitar and vocal to close proceedings, concluding an impressively dramatic performance.

'Everybody Knows (Except You)' (Hannon)

The obvious single choice from the album, this wonderful pop tune became a Top 20 hit single and deservedly so. Using the same trick as The Beatles' 1964 single 'Can't Buy Me Love' – opening with a catchy chorus – it consolidated The Divine Comedy's reputation as a consistent hit singles act, spending a month on the chart in the spring of 1997. The simple chorus, played on piano, has a lovely rising melody line that soon imprints on the brain, making it one of those tunes you can't resist singing along with. The verses sound very Burt Bacharach-influenced but remain harmonically uncomplicated, making for a perfect pop song. The sympathetic strings amplify the romantic mood of the song as it progresses. A brief Hannon guitar solo appears in the middle of the song, which is short, to the point and very effective.

Lyrically, he sounds desperate, as his loved one won't acknowledge the fact that he's madly in love with her, so instead, he tells the world and his wife of his longing for her, eventually driving all his friends 'round the bend' with his constant amorous reiterations. Not content with this, he then harangues 'passers-by' with his lovelorn lamentation to the extent that he admits, 'I made a small boy cry'. Towards the end of the song, we are left in no doubt of his desire, as he touchingly pleads his case to her over the chorus chord sequence. For the last two lines of the final chorus, the arrangement falls back to just Hannon's vocal and some subtle orchestration to close this impeccable pop tune. The single was issued in three formats: CD1 (red), CD2 (orange) and CD3 (green), all with added live tracks taken from gigs. The most interesting of these was CD2, which included a cover version of the Mark Eitzel song 'Johnny Mathis' Feet', originally recorded by The American Music Club and released on their 1993 album *Mercury*.

'Someone' (Hannon)

This towering ballad has a similar rhythmic tempo to Phil Spector's 1964 production 'You've Lost That Lovin' Feeling' – a transatlantic number-one hit for The Righteous Brothers. Hannon croons fetchingly against a big orchestral backdrop on the melodic verses, which are separated by a strident, reverb-drenched guitar figure. It's the kind of tune that you could imagine someone like Matt Monro having a go at back in the 1960s. There is also a hint of the Jerome Kern/Otto Harbach standard 'Smoke Gets In Your Eyes' about the melody. In lieu of a chorus, the verses end with a slow, chromatic descent, with a chord change on each word of Hannon's lyric line – 'I – need – to – be someone's somebody' – then we're back to the shimmering guitar figure that links the verses. It's the intense, brooding atmosphere that carries this love song and it builds up into a huge-sounding track towards the end, with the orchestral strings and brass displaying an almost overbearing intensity. This inflated arrangement evinces a rather hollow feel at its core, though, akin to that of an over-inflated meringue, full of air. Perhaps the lack of a strong lead instrumental line in this section contributes to this effect, as it is all big orchestral chords without a top-line melody to give it more interest. It does, however, fall back down to a quieter coda of just the repeated, reverberating guitar figure heard earlier, bringing things to an elegant close.

'If...' (Hannon)
Not to be confused with the much-covered David Gates standard of the same name or Rudyard Kipling's famous poem, this track is one of the most enigmatic of Hannon's love songs. In its odd but strangely moving lyric, he compares his loved one with many different things and ponders on how he would still show his love in these imaginary scenarios. Some of the 'If you were' comparisons are very unusual, including a tree, a man, a horse and a dog. It's a lyric that points toward obsession and is, for that reason, quite unsettling in places. It does make for weirdly compelling listening, though. Interestingly, Hannon's favoured species – horses and dogs – are again invoked, as they are on several other tracks from this album.

The vocal is backed by some John Lennon, *Imagine*-style piano, opening on a major chord, with sympathetic orchestral decoration. It revolves around a deliciously simple sequence that lends the affecting melody considerable gravitas, with an undertow of sadness. After the second 'If you were a horse' line, the music modulates to a new sequence, starting on a minor chord. This change perfectly evokes the image of a horse and rider, heading out over the fields. The original chord progression then resumes for an instrumental break and another verse, before a dramatic and unexpected coda, following the second 'If you were my dog' line, where the piano and orchestra stab relentlessly on an unsettling diminished seventh chord. In this closing section, Hannon elaborates on the benefits of being his 'loyal four-legged friend' and remaining 'together till the end', leaving this odd but galvanising track floating in mid-air on an unresolved suspension.

'If I Were You (I'd Be Through With Me)' (Hannon)
Written on a bus journey whilst returning from the Edinburgh Festival in late summer 1994, Hannon dusted off this older song for inclusion on the album. The lyric explores a blurring of the lines between masculine and feminine, with Hannon attempting to put himself in his partner's shoes, seeming to be in awe of her ability to put up with his less desirable traits and habits. By the time the elating chorus rolls around, the lyrics have become more ambiguous, and it's uncertain as to whether he is addressing his partner or one of his beloved horses when he sings of riding away and grazing on 'The grass so succulent and sweet'.

The rhythm of the song displays a Latin influence and the line, 'Just break on through', sounds like a nod to The Doors' Jim Morrison; perhaps no coincidence, as the rhythmic thrust of the song is almost identical to that of The Doors' 1968 hit single 'Light My Fire'. A piano figure links the verses and those wondrous, expansive choruses conjure visions of the wide, open prairie. This is especially true of the expanded final chorus, which has a really strong American, Mid-Western feel (something that Hannon would explore again on future albums). For me, that breathtaking chorus really makes this song.

'Timewatching' (Hannon)
This is a remake of one of Hannon's much older songs, dating from the 1990 EP *Timewatch*. The arrangement here is similar to that employed on the version recorded for *Liberation*. The main difference is the use of more violins and violas and less cello, making this a slightly more expansive-sounding arrangement. The song still evinces its overwhelming mournful vibe despite its lyrical and musical brilliance, but I'm not sure if it was really the perfect fit for this particular album. It does feel a bit like the odd track out on this collection and was a better fit for the concept on *Liberation*.

'I'm All You Need' (Hannon)
Originally attempted for inclusion on *Casanova*, this particular ditty didn't make the grade on that occasion but was dusted off and re-recorded to close this rather short album. This is another song with a magnificent chorus and another that recalls those big ballads of the 1960s. The ghost of Scott Walker hovers somewhere in the vicinity again, making this Hannon's most Scott Walker-obsessed album yet, although his influence remained with him throughout The Divine Comedy's career. The sound of *A Short Album About Love* also reminds me of Ivor Raymonde's distinctive orchestral-pop arrangements for Dusty Springfield during the 1960s. A slurred guitar figure links the verses, in which the orchestra float gracefully behind the vocal, with a keening upper-octave, sustained strings and flute note holding in the background, creating a feeling of suspense – a Walker Brothers trademark back in the day. This tension is released as the glorious chorus arrives, advising us not to 'look a horse in the mouth' and then invoking (of all things) a frog 'Dragging you round like a dog on a lead', before the titular punchline. One final verse closes the album with Hannon crooning his everlasting love, getting quieter and quieter as the orchestra hold a sustained string chord over his fading voice, making for a perfect ending to the album.

Additional Material
'I've Been To A Marvellous Party' (Coward)
Written in 1938 by Noel Coward, this song was inspired by a party in the south of France, thrown by American gossip columnist Elsa Maxwell the previous year. It was written for Coward's 1939 Broadway revue *Set To Music*. Hannon gives an interesting reading of the song, starting in true Noel Coward style with tinkling piano and a recited lyric. This morphs into an incongruous late 1990s techno dance-style, drum and bass arrangement, owing a debt to Underworld's 'Born Slippy' – as the party becomes more of a rave. The most

amusing bit of the arrangement for me is towards the end, when it briefly returns to a more traditional Coward-like mode, with a sped-up final flourish of 'Ha ha! I couldn't have liked it more!'

It all makes for quite a fun performance and is very different from Hannon's more familiar style signifiers – a bit of a one-off, really. On the single, it was paired with another more traditionally styled Coward cover of 'Someday I'll Find You', performed by Shola Ama and Craig Armstrong. The resulting number 28 UK hit single raised funds for *The Red Hot AIDS Charitable Trust*. 'Marvellous Party' also featured on the DC compilation album *A Secret History...The Best of The Divine Comedy*.

Fin De Siecle (1998)

Neil Hannon: vocals, guitar
Ivor Talbot: guitar
Bryan Mills: bass
Joby Talbot: piano, harpsichord
Stuart 'Pinkie' Bates: organ, accordion
Miggy Barradas: drums
Rob Farrer: percussion
Hilary Summers: vocals ('Sweden', 'Commuter Love')
Dexter Fletcher: narration ('Here Comes The Flood')
Steve Hilton: programming ('Eric The Gardener')
The Brunel Ensemble:
Christopher George, Maya Bickel, Kate Birchall, Benjamin Harte, Bernice Lavigne, Mary Martin, Benjamin Nabarro, Roy Theaker: violin 1
Charles Mutter, Arousssiak Baltaian, Eos Counsell, Anna Giddey, Kelly McCusker, Emma Mitchell, Timothy Myall, Matthew Ward: violin 2
Yannick Dondelinger, David Aspin, Joanna Lacey, Jong On Lau, John Murphy, Robert Riley: viola
Betsy Taylor, Emmeline Brewer, Christopher Fish, Louise Hopkins, Robbie Jacobs: cello
Peter Devlin, Philip Dawson, Ian Watson: double bass
Rebecca Larson: flute, alto flute, piccolo
Max Spiers: oboe, cor anglais
Charlotte Glasson: soprano saxophone, tenor saxophone, baritone saxophone, flute
Chris Caldwell: alto saxophone
Kevin Christiane: tenor saxophone
Stuart King: clarinet, bass clarinet
Simon Haram: soprano saxophone
Rebecca Menday: bassoon
Matthew Gunner, Tansy Davies, Jonathan Morcombe, Jonathan Hassan: horn
Daniel Newell, Mark Law, Robert Samuel: trumpet
Simon Jones: trumpet, piccolo trumpet
Tom Hammond: trombone
Andrew Harwood-White: bass trombone
Simon Roberts: tuba
Lucy Wakeford: harp
Chris Austin: artistic director
Deborah Keyser: administration
Crouch End Festival Chorus:
David Temple: chorus master
Rachel Conner, Denise Haddon, Gisela Soinne, Nina Weiss, Julia White, Jenny Watson, Pamela Constantinou, Pat Whitehead, Liz Knight, Sue McCrone, Alison Mason, Naomi Fulop, Felicity Ford: sopranos

Alison Brister, Tina Burnett-Pope, Jo Chapman, Veronica Gray, Rhael Jenkins, Elise Golden, Jane Heliwell, Pauline Hoyle, Catherine Best, Maggie Huntingford, Claire Turner: altos
Michael Coates, John Best, Steve McAdam, Ken Wilson, Nick Turner, Philip Robinson, Christopher Higgs, Barry Varley-Tipton: tenors
Roger Cleave, Geoff Kembell-Cook, Robert Goodall, Paul Haddon, Martin Hudson, Bruce Boyd, Vincent Lawler, Paul Mason, Lenny Fagin, Stephen Greenway, Ian Lawrence, John Gibbons, Matthew Turner: basses
Recorded at September Sound, The Dairy and Olympic Studios, London between 13 March and 2 April 1998
Mixed at Westpoint Studios, London
Producer: Jon Jacobs
Co-producer: Neil Hannon
Engineer: Jon Jacobs
Additional Engineer: Andy Scade, assisted by Mitsuo Tate, Adam Brown and Mark Togashi
Record label: Setanta
Released: 31 August 1998
Highest UK chart position: 9

1997 proved to be a busy year for the core live unit of The Divine Comedy, with a full gig schedule. They were touring incessantly through the UK and Europe over the summer, including some continental dates supporting Radiohead and a combo gig with classical composer Michael Nyman at Flux, Edinburgh New Music Festival on 12 August. Nyman's influence had permeated Hannon's music since *Liberation* and, particularly, *Promenade*. It's worth noting that Hannon covered several Michael Nyman compositions: 'Time Lapse' (included on the single 'Generation Sex' CD1), 'Chasing Sheep Is Best Left To Shepherds' (on 'Generation Sex' CD2), 'Miranda' (on 'The Certainty Of Chance' CD1) and 'Knowing The Ropes' (on 'The Certainty Of Chance' CD2).

In December, percussionist Rob Farrer joined The Divine Comedy and on 15 January 1998, they took part in a concert dubbed *The 20th Century Blues Gala Evening – A Tribute To Noel Coward*, along with Suede, Pet Shop Boys, Elton John, Sting, Robbie Williams and Marianne Faithful. The DC contribution was Hannon's arrangement of Noel Coward's 'I've Been To A Marvellous Party'. It was the featured DC track on the compilation album *Twentieth Century Blues – The Songs of Noel Coward*, released in April 1998.

On 13 March, The Divine Comedy commenced recording for the new album *Fin De Siecle* at The Dairy Studios, London and these sessions ran through to 2 April. Following this, between 4 and 6 April, Hannon jetted off to Vienna with photographer Kevin Westenberg to capture images for the new album's cover artwork. The front cover photo is a monochrome, head-and-shoulders, sideways profile shot of Neil Hannon standing alongside a memorial monument; further shots taken at this location were used for the rear and inside cover artwork.

Released on 31 August to mixed reviews from the press, *Fin De Siecle* proved to be an ambitious beast. With the largest orchestral forces yet garnered for a DC album at his disposal, Neil Hannon, with assistance from his sidekick Joby Talbot and producer Jon Jacobs (chosen because he had worked with ELO maestro Jeff Lynne – one of Hannon's adolescent favourites), created this imposing collection of sonic landscapes. The lyrics generally address sweeping, historical themes compared to Hannon's previously more personal tack. The lyrics are laced with large doses of pessimism and black humour but balanced with some flickers of optimism. Although the *Melody Maker* reviewer praised the finished product as 'A record dangerously close to a masterpiece', many other reviewers weren't quite so keen. Neil Spencer in *The Observer* reckoned that '*Fin De Siecle* sags beneath the weight of its millennial concept' and a clutch of other negative reviews perhaps demonstrated that The Divine Comedy were no longer 'flavour of the month' with certain cynical sections of the music press.

To my ears, this is one of Hannon's most engaging albums, albeit with sizeable doses of doom-mongering and a preoccupation with death permeating many tracks. Chances are, had this album appeared a couple of decades earlier, it would probably have been lumped in with progressive rock – such is the awe-inspiring orchestral scale of its construction and execution. Reviews notwithstanding, the general public voted with their hard-earned cash and *Fin De Siecle* sailed up to number nine in the UK album charts, during an impressive 16-week run, over the closing months of 1998. This was no doubt helped by the fact that there were three hit singles from the album, including 'National Express', which penetrated the UK Top Ten, peaking at number eight over the spring of 1999 to become The Divine Comedy's biggest hit single of the 1990s. This album also marked the end of Hannon's contract with Setanta Records, who had done him proud through the 1990s.

'Generation Sex' (Hannon)

This beat-driven and cannily orchestrated song comments on society's general attitudes towards women. Samples from a Katie Puckrick talk show both open the track and appear in the middle section, where the momentum slows for a while. Opening with some touching oboe lines, the forward thrust of the song is enhanced by two dramatic timpani beats per bar and a slipstream of plucked harp arpeggios that glide through the second verse. The melody is engaging and wide-ranging, with a streamlined feel that propels the track ever forward, supported by the strong orchestral forces at hand.

The lyrics range from comments on the public perception of female nudity to the paparazzi, with their 'telephoto lenses' as they 'chase Mercedes Benz's' – recalling the then-recent death of Princess Diana. After a further lyrical sideswipe at cosmetic surgery, the song builds to its climax and Hannon unleashes an emotive guitar solo that sticks close to the verse melody, with dramatic orchestration building around it. This combination really drives the track towards the powerful rhythmic punctuations that hammer it to a close. Released as the first single from the album, it peaked at number 19 on the UK chart in September 1998.

'Thrillseeker' (Hannon)

Leading off with some trilling flute, 'Thrillseeker' then launches into a hammering snare drum and powerful guitar riff, couched within dramatic orchestration. You can easily imagine this track being used as a film theme song for a spy thriller. The music that makes up the verse conjures up a strong Iberian feel with its rhythm and melody, as Flamenco-style accents imbue the music with high drama. The choruses increase the melodrama, returning to the A to Dm6 chord shifts heard in the intro. The music quite literally paints a vivid picture of peril on an icy mountainside.

Lyrically, this is a song for adrenaline junkies everywhere and the action is set on a difficult-to-conquer peak (possibly in the Pyrenees, judging by the Catalonian flavour of the music!). The lyrics are full of the usual Hannon wit and wisdom, with some glorious couplets to savour, including a touch of conceptual continuity in the first verse. While cogitating on the strange things that go through your head when faced with an imminent demise, Hannon throws in a tongue-in-cheek reference to one of his earlier songs, pondering, 'What was in that woodshed? – Will death be gentle?' (the woodshed in question being the one mentioned in the song 'Something For The Weekend' from the *Casanova* album). This initial verse also quotes Confucius, the ancient Chinese philosopher, to provide the deliciously witty couplet: 'Better to live one day, like a lion than, a thousand sheepishly' say, dead oriental'. His rhyming scheme in this verse is a master class in clever lyric writing.

Following the first of the catchy choruses, buoyed by orchestra and concerto-like piano chords, there is an effective employment of a vocal processor to echo the phrase 'Thrill-seeker', as if the sound is reverberating across a valley between two mountain peaks. Simultaneously, a falling melody line glides downhill like a descending skier, morphing into a solo on synthesiser that is reminiscent of the style of ELP keyboardist Keith Emerson. The big production occasionally falls back to just a glockenspiel and flute figure for two bars, displaying an impressive sense of dynamics.

Hannon reflects on those who put their life in peril in the cause of adrenaline-kicks, some of whom inevitably 'Reap their reward' of 'death by faulty ripcord, or loose carabina'. The final verse finds our bold protagonist stuck halfway up a mountain and 'frying under the sun', while emergency services spend a fortune attempting a rescue, 'albeit vainly' as the lyric runs. One final rousing chorus is accompanied by an icy wind whipping across the sheer mountainside, as our hapless adventurer laughs in the face of an imminent demise, no doubt feeling more alive in that dangerous moment than in many a humdrum day, as experienced by most mortals. To close proceedings, the track dynamically dips back to just the flute and glockenspiel, to complete an impressive track.

'Commuter Love' (Hannon)

Opening to the strains of Stuart 'Pinkie' Bates' accordion, this feels very Parisian-like from the off. Taken at a dead slow tempo, Joby Talbot's piano backing accompanies Hannon's smooth vocalisations, as he describes a romantic fantasy enacted whilst on a tube train commuter run, possibly on the Paris Metro, judging by the European vibe of the melody and arrangement. The station sounds, however, were recorded at London Waterloo.

Lyrically, it encapsulates that moment when you might see an attractive person on a train journey and fantasise about them. In the case of this song, the near-obsessive behaviour of the protagonist veers perilously close to making it a 'stalking' song. The later verses, however, clarify the more romantic intent at work here, as the chorus explains. Although she doesn't know he exists, he wants to 'keep it like this'. Following this first chorus, there is a sudden tempo change with a tom-tom rhythm and an ascending orchestral build-up. However, this vanishes as quickly as it appears, reverting back to a slow tempo for the second verse. In the slightly rearranged second chorus, our protagonist denies being obsessed, claiming he doesn't want to 'see her undressed' but just to imagine they are 'prince and princess' in his dreams. Hannon's vocal in this section is answered by the female soprano voice of Hilary Summers, echoing the words 'in my dreams'. He then unleashes one of his most emotionally charged, but carefully arranged guitar solos yet, and like many of the instrumental outbursts on this album, it appears to ascend into the heavens before falling back to a repeat of the first chorus and the return of the Parisian accordion riff. This fades back into the station public address-system train announcements heard earlier, closing a magnificently moody performance.

'Sweden' (Hannon)

One of the most dramatic tracks on a suspenseful album, this tribute to the land of Ikea, Abba and Volvo quite literally kicks off, with the orchestral brass and strings initiating a timpani-laden, goose-stepping rhythm that defines high drama. With an unrelenting minor-key construction, this chilly arrangement perfectly evokes a snowy Scandinavian landscape, as Hannon waxes eloquently on his love of all things Swedish. The verses are taken at the relaxed pace of a gentle Husky-powered Troika ride through the pines, followed by the towering choruses, where Hannon chants the title, with Hilary Summers' spectral soprano reply-vocal sounding as ghostly as a wailing Valkyrie. The Crouch End Chorus provide further backing, as they chant 'Sverige' (the native name for Sweden) in the background. This is all set against a return of the stiffly marching stride of the orchestral intro, and the bombast of this arrangement is almost operatic in its intensity. Hannon's lyric delivers a list of his Scandinavian heroes: film director Ingmar Bergman, artist Karin Larsson, Nina Persson – lead singer of Swedish band The Cardigans – and one Norwegian: the 19th-century playwright Henrik Ibsen, who sneaks into the list! That intense marching orchestral intro returns once more to close the track, with a melodramatic, staccato punctuation that feels akin to skiing off the edge of a musical precipice and into thin air.

'Eric The Gardener' (Hannon, Talbot)

This, the longest track on the album – clocking in at 8:24 – is based on the true story of Eric Lawes, a retired gardener who, whilst undertaking a spot of metal detecting on his friend Peter Watkins' farm in Hoxne, Suffolk, in 1992, inadvertently uncovered a vast Roman treasure trove. This expansive track opens to the sound of a metal detector, prior to the entry of a minimalist-inspired, repeating six-note piano figure in a 5/4 time signature that forms the basis of the entire track. Hannon's simple vocal melody follows that of the piano riff and the track exudes a laconic 5/4 drift that becomes more hypnotic as it progresses. After the first verse, Joby Talbot's orchestral arrangement arrives, suggesting implied sixth, minor seventh and flattened fifth chords against the unchanging piano riff that, when combined with Hannon's lyrics and sung melody, cast a beguiling spell.

Lyrically, the song explores the notion of deep time, with a sense of drift that appears to take us back several millennia and links the time of Julius Caesar to the present day. Hannon invokes the aforementioned Emperor of Rome who came, saw and conquered the damp, drizzly British Isles, only to leave again after 'too many sniffs and colds, got up his Roman nose'. However, despite Caesar leaving it all behind, something of his legacy would remain 'buried deep in English slime' to be unearthed by Eric the Gardener a few thousand years down the line. The song casts Eric as a sort of Everyman figure, representing the common working man, and is really a comment on that 'great leveller': death itself – the powerful emperor and his like, being no more mighty in the face of eternity than good old Eric!

After several verses, we encounter a massive, ascending orchestral build-up that seems to shift us through a temporal vortex into a third verse, before depositing us into a floating melange of drifting orchestral chords and electronica, reminiscent in style to early 1970s Tangerine Dream. The 5/4 rhythm is grounded by a pulsing bass drum beat that underpins this section, while the 5/4 riff now has an identical bass riff reflecting it, but rhythmically offset by a beat, evoking a canon-like effect. Miggy Barradas' snare drum work in this section is particularly noteworthy. This remarkable track finally returns to the lone piano riff before satisfyingly resolving on an orchestral minor chord, concluding a stunning piece of arranging. A shorter, acoustic guitar-based version of this song was included on the 1999 single 'The Pop Singer's Fear Of The Pollen Count' and is also well worth a listen.

'National Express' (Hannon)
Next up, it's the joker in the pack – a moment of light relief among the darker and deeper tracks on the album. This ebullient swinger won over the general public on its release as a single in early 1999. The big-band brass swing of the intro cleverly introduces what will later become the sequence for the wordless vocal chants, providing the all-join-in, catchy choruses. Rhythm guitar and jangle-piano provide the loose-limbed verses with an irresistible, swinging beat, as Hannon croons smoothly in praise of the British transport system. Although the title is a paean to the well-known coach company of the same name and there is a lyrical reference to the 'jolly hostess' – I don't personally recall encountering one of these on any of my numerous National Express coach trips through the years!

The lyrics contain some razor-sharp observations on human behaviour as we encounter the feeble old dear, the screaming child, the student and the family man ('manhandling the pram with paternal pride') – as Hannon puts it: 'All human life is here'. Those memorable chorus chants of, 'everybody sing: ba-ba-ba-da, ba-ba-ba-da', ensured the popularity of the single with its all-inclusive invitation to sing along. A lyrical reference to the voluminous derriere of the aforementioned jolly hostess would undoubtedly be deemed non-PC these days, though! There's a nice touch in the backing vocals on the second verse, too, following a mention of the hostess' wedding 'back in '63'; the backing vocal chant of 'yeah, yeah, yeah, yeah' recalls that era's then omnipresent Fab Four. Preceding the lengthy instrumental coda, Hannon whips out his megaphone and makes a clarion call to the populace, inviting them to roll up for the trip – much as The Beatles did in 1967 on 'Magical Mystery Tour'. The coda swings off into the sunset, with Hannon chanting the song title over and over whilst an excellent, bluesy piano solo – presumably played by Joby Talbot – is joined by some deft flute improvisation to take the track home, ending a worthy Top-Ten hit.

The single was issued in three formats: CD1 included an acoustic version of 'Going Downhill Fast' and a cover of Kraftwerk's 'Radioactivity'; CD2 featured the Stephin Merritt song 'Famous' (a reflection on the nature of fame) and 'Overstrand' (a Noel Coward-type piano-led song, and a caustic comment on ambition and the lengths some people will go to acquire riches); the final format issued was a cassette single which included a variation on the *Fin De Siecle* track 'Sweden' with different lyrics, entitled 'The Heart Of Rock And Roll' (a song about how the untalented can become famous overnight).

'Life On Earth' (Hannon)
Opening with another dose of Parisian accordion from Stuart Bates, the continental feel so prevalent on this album is maintained. A bolero-like snare drum rhythm graces the slowly moving verses of this sad, melodic song of resignation. The accordion riff returns between the verses and on the fade-out of this track. Hannon's funereal lyrics dip into French for the odd line,

as he croons, 'Au revoir joie, bonjour tristesse' ('farewell joy, hello sadness' in English) and laments our eventual, inevitable exit from this corporeal world. Also dismissing belief in superstition with the proviso, 'Don't rely on the starry sky', he advises the listener: 'Try to live your life on Earth'. Despite its mournful ambience, this beautiful and melancholic melody proves to be strangely uplifting.

'The Certainty Of Chance' (Hannon, Talbot)
Joby Talbot arranged this co-creation with Neil Hannon, which proceeds with a slow-paced orchestral grandeur, enhanced by prominent timpani and snare drumbeats crossing the bar lines. Hannon's lyric reflects on the notion of 'chaos theory' – how extremely small things can affect the bigger picture, including the classic example of the so-called 'butterfly effect'. The first verse conjures the proverbial butterfly flapping its wings and starting an exponential chain reaction that eventually builds into a hurricane, while the second verse has a tech-wizard schoolboy hitting 'return' on his computer and causing the worldwide web to 'crash and burn'. The final verse reverts to a more personal tack, as Hannon appears to be addressing a relationship issue rather than the more universal topics in previous verses. Another song about inevitability, it continues the philosophical musing that is so much part of this album.

Musically, there are some fascinating touches to this song's arrangement: the piano cascades in the choruses move through a major, minor seventh to augmented chord sequence that feels odd and unusual, accentuating the doom-laden quality of the lyrics. There is some beautiful, lush orchestral work in evidence, especially on the lengthy coda, including a possibly unconscious nod to the feel of the incidental music used on the 1960s TV series *Thunderbirds*, especially the prominent flute run that is underpinned with some tasty suspended and diminished chords. It is a passage that evokes the atmospheric soundtrack employed in the aforementioned puppet show whenever arch-villain The Hood makes an appearance to try and thwart the Tracy brothers' efforts to preserve life. To close the track, Hannon wanted to use a sample of speech in Italian from the 1960 Fellini film *La Dolce Vita*, but was denied permission from the Fellini Foundation, so instead, recited the English subtitles of this passage over the closing orchestral backdrop. It advises us to live in a state of enchantment and remain detached. Despite appearing as an unusual choice for a single, this song managed to climb to number 49 in the UK chart when it was released as such in November 1998.

'Here Comes The Flood' (Hannon)
Not to be confused with Peter Gabriel's 1977 song of the same name, this Hannon original is a very different beast. Coming on like the theme song to a stage musical about the end of the world, the arrangement is very 'Broadway' (meant in a tongue-in-cheek way). The swinging, triple-time rhythm is driven by piano and builds to cinematic-overkill proportions as it progresses. With

a big orchestral backup, this track is something of a monster, reflecting lyrics that ponder the disintegration of society. Also dipping into cinematic science-fiction, it evokes disasters (both real and imagined) – including earthquakes, fire, floods, rivers of mud, a fifty-foot fly and even the 'race from outer space' – as it explodes into a mass of screams, explosions and some convincing Star Wars-style laser sound effects, accompanied by a suitably doom-evoking orchestral soundtrack. This depiction of the ultimate disaster movie eventually falls back to a smoother piano and vibes backing, with Dexter Fletcher's American TV-styled narration of the afflictions affecting and obsessing the human race at the dawn of the millennium. It's an authentic evocation of American TV tuned in to CNN or some such, and after one more not-so-cheery chorus, the track closes with a lone piano and a howling wind.

'Sunrise' (Hannon)
The one truly personal song on this collection, this is Hannon singing from the heart. The song reflects on his childhood in strife-torn Ulster and how he managed to survive it both physically and mentally. As mentioned in passing in an earlier chapter, it was no doubt inspired by his proximity to the IRA bombing of Enniskillen on 8 November 1987 and the later cause for hope signalled by the signing of the Good Friday Agreement on 10 April 1998. The initial verses reflect on Hannon's younger life in Londonderry and Enniskillen, set to a lilting triple-time tune of great charm, resembling a gentle lullaby. It is accompanied by a spinet-like keyboard sound, buoyed by lush orchestration. The mood is split by a remarkable, ascending vocal by Hannon, pushing to the very top of his extraordinary range, as he reflects on the political and religious dogma that underlies such needless human suffering. A 'Who cares?' tirade, that covers governance, the naming of towns and national borders, climaxes with the line, 'Who'll care when you're six feet beneath the ground?' The last held note of this line demonstrates what an amazingly flexible voice he possesses and also his skill at voice control. It's an intensely moving moment, especially as the song moves into its final, hymn-like verses that invoke a metaphorical sunrise of hope. Capping one of his best-ever vocal performances, the final repeated chants of 'It's the sunrise' bring tears to my eyes on every listen. It's one of the true peaks in the DC canon of music – both passionate and beautiful; it closes a remarkable album.

Additional Material
'London Irish' (Hannon)
A mid-tempo strummed acoustic guitar accompanies Neil Hannon's vocals on the first verse of this tribute to his fellow Irishmen who migrated to London. The guitar is joined by accordion chords as the track progresses. The accordion rhythm changes to the offbeat on later verses and the arrangement is kept simple all the way through, falling back to just strummed guitar for a while before the accordion returns once more.

Back in the 1990s, Hannon was one of the 'London Irish' who had traditionally come over from the Emerald Isle over the years to seek their fortune, no doubt in search of the mythical gold-paved streets of the UK capital. The song was written during that period. There are some touching couplets for those who have Irish blood in their veins and the lyrics find Hannon pondering if success will cause him to lose some of his Irish traits. This preoccupation eventually saw him move back to Ireland in 2003 – first to Dublin and later to Kildare. His vocals shift up an octave towards the end of the song, racking up the emotion, before it ends on a held accordion chord. This song appeared on the 'Generation Sex' CD1 single, released on 14 September 1998.

'Little Acts Of Kindness' (Hannon)

This track was originally included on the 'Generation Sex' CD2 single. The verses move between major seventh and minor seventh chords with a light, samba-like shuffle, while the uplifting chorus reverts to a major key. It sees Neil Hannon reflecting on amity and kind-heartedness, delivering a let's-be-nice-to-each-other plea that sends out a strong, positive, feel-good vibe. The lyrics are both heartfelt and, in places, mildly amusing, as he lists some of the nice day-to-day things you can do for others, including donating your last Rolo to a friend, making cups of coffee or 'feeding horses Polos'. The chorus clarifies why it's good and right to show kindness to others, especially if they are going through a hard time as, let's face it, 'We've all been there before'.

'Postcards To Rosie' (Hannon)

This delicate, largely acoustic song was written for Neil Hannon's niece Rosie. Acoustic guitar arpeggios create an intimate atmosphere, as Hannon sings of his promise to send postcards to Rosie from various ports of call around the globe, including the alliterative destinations 'Paris, Paraguay, Prague and Peru' and even a postcard 'from Liverpool, if Beirut and Baghdad won't do'. As a second picked acoustic guitar joins in, it reminds me of the work of the late, great Freddie Phillips and his charming songs featured in the 'Trumptonshire Trilogy' of children's TV programmes, created by animator Gordon Murray in the 1960s (*Camberwick Green*, *Trumpton* and *Chigley*).

In the final verse, Hannon begs forgiveness from Rosie for those times he forgets to send her a postcard, assuring her: 'I'll make you proud of me yet'. This track first appeared on the 7" single release of 'Generation Sex' on 14 September 1998.

'Last Stand In Metroland' (Hannon)

Two chords of staccato electric guitar set up a metronomic rhythm, joined by bass and thumping snare drum, kicking off this interesting song. It has a kind of robotic Kraftwerk feel to it, in common with several DC tracks from this period.

There have been several fanciful interpretations of the lyrics of 'Last Stand In Metroland' put forward by fans, basing the action around the World War Two period. However, I think it is pretty clear from the lyrics that this song is rather another sympathetic alignment with the more current green movement, as the protagonist and his companion appear to be an eco-warrior father and son duo. They have their obvious differences but seem to agree on making a stand on this one issue. There are some tasty lyrical couplets, including 'I live in Osterley, you live in a tree' and 'You're somewhere left of Marx, I fancy Alan Clarke', but despite their lifestyle and political differences, 'when the diggers start, we both cry'. The chorus title chant is bolstered by some one-note rhythmic piano that helps propel the track along and there is a touch of phasing on the vocals. The chorus chanting becomes almost hypnotic on the long fade-out.

'The Dead Only Quickly' (Merritt)

This DC cover version was written by Stephin Merritt and was originally released in 1996 by The Gothic Archies on their EP *Looming In The Gloom*. Neil Hannon's cover version was first featured on 'The Certainty Of Chance' CD2 single, released on 9 November 1998. It may be a short track, clocking in at 1:14, but it packs quite a lyrical punch. It takes the view that, although 'Priests and fools say, we are but animate clay', the only thing we can really be sure of is that we eventually return to dust. The darkly amusing chorus-chant claims of the dead: 'They don't go about being born and reborn and rising and falling like souffle', but instead, 'The dead only quickly decay'.

The DC arrangement cleverly employs just two saxophones, panned out towards the sides of the stereo picture, sounding like a baritone sax on one side and a soprano sax on the other side, with Hannon's rich vocal tones sandwiched in between. The effect is darkly comical and this short slice of black humour is up there with my all-time personal favourite DC recordings – it's a wondrous little gem.

'Maryland Electric Rainstorm' (Hannon)

Opening with a Kraftwerk-inspired electronic shimmering effect, this scintillating pulse recurs throughout the track, lending it a distinctive atmosphere. It also fits with the lyric, in which the subject of the song, Amory Blaine, takes a supposed shortcut through a forest in Maryland, USA and is caught in an electric storm. Blaine is a central character in F. Scott Fitzgerald's 1920 novel *This Side Of Paradise*. As the forest gives way to fields of hay bales, the protagonist hears a husky female voice singing the poem 'Les sanglots des violins d'automne'. This poem was the work of French Symbolist poet Paul-Marie Verlaine and was first published in 1866. Blaine subsequently charms the woman and they join hands as the electric storm continues to rage above them, soaking them through.

The music circles around an insistent four-chord sequence, as it builds and the story unfolds; the strong atmosphere carries the arrangement admirably, making for an intriguingly entrancing listening experience. It first appeared on the cassette version of the single 'The Certainty Of Chance' on 9 November 1998.

'With Whom To Dance' (Merritt)

There was definitely something of a mutual admiration society going on between Neil Hannon and Stephin Merritt, as The Divine Comedy covered several Merritt songs throughout the 1990s and Hannon appeared as a guest with another Merritt band, The 6ths, on their album *Hyacinths & Thistles*, released on 18 September 2000. This album included a piano version of 'The Dead Only Quickly', performed by Hannon.

The original recording of 'With Whom To Dance' by The Magnetic Fields was from their 1995 album *Get Lost*. The DC cover version first appeared on 'The Pop Singer's Fear Of The Pollen Count' single, released on 9 August 1999. It's a charming song, based mainly on major chords and performed in a fetching triple-time arrangement of churning acoustic guitars and the atmospheric accordion-playing of Stuart 'Pinkie' Bates. Hannon puts on his best crooning voice for this simple plea for someone 'With Whom To Dance'. The middle eight is truly gorgeous, as Hannon croons, 'You look like heaven, an angel who stepped from a dream', with the imaginative rhyme, 'Seven-hundred and seventy-seven times lovelier, than anything I've ever seen'. This track is another buried gem and is well worth seeking out.

'Gin Soaked Boy' (Hannon)

This single deserved better than the number 38 peak it reached in the UK chart in November 1999. Also included on the compilation album *A Secret History* that year, this hypnotic song is driven along by churning acoustic guitars and keyboard arpeggios, with a hint of the Bo Diddley beat. It also employs the poetic device of anaphora to give added emphasis to the statements made in the lyrics – every line beginning with the words 'I'm the...'. This gives the impression that the succession of images evoked feel, in some way, more profound. It's a delicious little exercise and the changing chords under melodic variations of its simple but memorable hook make for an invigorating listen.

'I Am' (Hannon, Eno)

The lyrics to 'I Am' are taken from the Brian Eno book *A Year With Swollen Appendices* and Hannon's music here is positively tribal, employing a drone (as used in much Indian music) and what sounds like a swarmandal (as played by George Harrison on The Beatles' 'Strawberry Fields Forever'). A tabla beat completes the illusion that we're somewhere on the Indian sub-continent and Hannon's vocals are recorded with a large degree of distortion. The lyrics list all the things that Eno felt defined him as a human being, and the one phrase returned to more than once is, 'I am a mammal'. It's a song of affirmation in being part of the primitive and basic circle of life, where we humans are just an adaption like any other on the planet. The song makes for an interesting little exercise in working around a one-chord drone. This track was released on 'Gin Soaked Boy' CD1 on 1 November 1999.

'Too Young To Die' (Hannon)
Added to the compilation album *A Secret History...The Best of The Divine Comedy*, 'Too Young To Die' is perhaps the track that most clearly presaged Neil Hannon's next phase after the excess of *Fin De Siecle*. It provided a clear pointer, both musically and lyrically, to the more stripped-down manifesto crystallised in the next DC album *Regeneration*. Taken at a slow tempo, Hannon's piano chords are accompanied by some rim shots, with a slow build to the fuller production emerging later in the song. There is some fairly muscular slide guitar, accompanied by a whooshing sound during the solo. The vocals are very Bowie-like, especially in the swaying choruses, where Hannon says goodbye to his suit, shirt and tie – in effect, closing his arty wardrobe and dressing down in preparation for musically touching base with his indie roots on the next project.

Regeneration (2001)

Personnel:
Neil Hannon: vocals, guitar, additional keyboards
Joby Talbot: piano, synthesiser, recorder, string arrangements
Ivor Talbot: guitar, additional bass
Stuart 'Pinkie' Bates: organ, synthesiser, trombone
Bryan Mills: bass
Miggy Barradas: drums, additional percussion
Rob Farrer: percussion
Everton Nelson: Millennia Strings – Leader ('Bad Ambassador', 'Lost Property', 'Mastermind' and 'The Beauty Regime')
Philip Sheppard: cello ('Perfect Lovesong')
Clio Gould: London TeleFilmonic Orchestra – Leader ('Note To Self')
Recorded at RAK Studios, London, mixed at Mayfair Studios, London and mastered at Abbey Road Studios, London by Chris Blair between July and November 2000
Producer: Nigel Godrich
Recording assistant: Dan Grech-Marguerat
Mixing assistant: Gerard Navarro
Record label: Parlophone
Released: 12 March 2001
Highest UK chart position: 14

1999 commenced with a tour supporting Robbie Williams, as The Divine Comedy promoted the single 'National Express', which ran through to March, by which time, the single was flying high in the UK Top Ten. In June, Hannon recorded a duet with Tom Jones: a cover of the Portishead song 'All Mine'. This was included on Tom Jones' *Reload* album, released on 17 September.

On 15 July, The Divine Comedy returned to Dublin to play support to none other than REM, who had proven so influential on the young Neil Hannon a decade earlier. In August, the band scored a further Top-20 hit single with a brass-driven remake of 'The Pop Singer's Fear Of The Pollen Count'. This single was issued in three formats: CD1 included a cover of Stephin Merritt's 'With Whom To Dance' and an acoustic take of 'Eric The Gardener'; CD2 featured a Hannon instrumental, 'This Side Of Paradise', with a cover version of Ride's 'Vapour Trails'; and the cassette format included a cover of Brel's 'Jackie'. On 30 August, Setanta released the classic DC compilation album *A Secret History...The Best Of The Divine Comedy*, which sailed up to number three in the UK album chart and spent an impressive 15 weeks on the listings. As well as nine previous UK hit singles, the album also contained a selection of Hannon's most famous album tracks, closing with the inevitable 'Tonight We Fly'. It also featured two previously unreleased tracks: 'Gin Soaked Boy' (which went on to be a further UK chart single in November) and 'Too Young To Die'. The release of *A Secret History* effectively drew a line under Hannon's decade-long tenure with Setanta Records, summing up a hugely creative and successful ten-year period for The Divine Comedy.

To cap a momentous year, Neil Hannon finally tied the knot with girlfriend Orla Little; their marriage ceremony took place at University Church, St. Stephen's Green, Dublin on 4 September 1999. While the newlywed couple honeymooned in Mexico, Hannon began writing songs for the next DC album.

As the new millennium dawned, the band performed a number of gigs in Scotland, where they road-tested the newest batch of Neil Hannon compositions in preparation for the recording sessions for *Regeneration*. Meanwhile, in March, the band performed on Ute Lemper's album *Punishing Kiss*, for which Neil Hannon and Joby Talbot had written a trio of new songs: 'The Case Continues', 'Split' and 'You Were Meant For Me'. With the termination of the Setanta deal, Hannon signed with a major label for the first time; his deal with Parlophone (the company that had famously signed The Beatles in 1962) was for a reputed one million pounds. On 3 July 2000, the band set up at RAK (Studio 1) in North London to commence recording for the new album. Hannon had decided to take a back-to-basics approach to the new project, going for a more stripped-down, indie-pop vibe, highlighting the seven-piece live line-up with less emphasis on orchestration than in the past. To this end, he deferred production duties to experienced producer Nigel Godrich, rather than produce the project himself. By the end of November, recording and mixing for the new album was completed.

This time around, the cover artwork was provided by Joby Talbot's wife, Claire Burbridge and was based on her sculpture designs of the human form in movement, tinted in yellows and browns. This made for a more abstract cover design than those employed for previous DC releases.

Regeneration was released on 12 March 2001 to a generally good reception from the media. Nigel Williamson in *The Times* called it 'A subtle collection of gorgeous pop songs', while John Mullen in *Mojo* observed its 'sombre musings with autumnal, string-filled exercises in restraint'. Over in America, never a major DC market, Gavin Edwards' review in *Rolling Stone* opined that the album displayed 'an exhausted loneliness all its own'. Radiohead producer Nigel Godrich certainly stripped down the sound on *Regeneration*, especially compared with the orchestral opulence of the previous DC album *Fin De Siecle*. Even Neil Hannon's visual appearance changed, as evidenced by the photos in the CD insert: long hair, jeans and T-shirt rather than the suits and shades of old.

Despite the major label promotion, *Regeneration* performed less well on the UK album chart than the previous three albums, managing a month on the listings, topping at number 14. Three singles emerged from the album and they were relatively minor hits compared with those taken from *Fin De Siecle*. The first, 'Love What You Do', charted in March 2001 and reached number 26. It was issued in three formats, with both CD2 and the cassette release including the Hannon song 'Get Me To A Monastery' (where he sounds like he's had enough of secular life and is ready to retreat!). The second single 'Bad Ambassador' made number 34 in May and was again a triple-format release, with CD2 and the cassette version featuring live tracks from gigs. A final single release from the album, 'Perfect Lovesong', struggled up to number 42, although it's a mystery why this gorgeous Beach Boys-influenced song didn't do better. This time, there was a choice of 2 CDs and a DVD version. CD2 had a further Hannon original tucked away in the shape of 'No Excuses' – a song urging action rather than apathy. He was reportedly disappointed with the sales figures of both the album and the singles, especially after the substantial chart success of a few years earlier. Artistically, *Regeneration* was a crucial album for him, though, and would prepare the way for a thrust forward into the new century, where The Divine Comedy would thrive musically for many years to come.

'Timestretched' (Hannon)

This song is a philosophical reflection on one of Hannon's favourite subjects, in that it concerns the relentless passing of time. Pondering the difficulty of finding sufficient time for creative endeavour, the lyrics mourn the fact that there are seemingly not enough hours in the day – days in the week, weeks in the month and months in the year – and that years disappear 'like the bubbles in my beer'. It carries the essence of thoughtful contemplation in a public house environment, after downing a few jars at the local. The pub references abound as the song progresses, Hannon ruminating on the barmen, knowing 'extracts from Carmen' (in reference to the Bizet opera of that name). The second verse meditates on the creative limitations of the art of musical composition with another string of not-enoughs. These include lines on the stave, notes in the scale and beats in the bar – the last-mentioned of these leads into the final lyrical pub analogy with the couplet, 'But bars get too busy, with folks asking is he...', followed by a mumbled, 'that guy – oh, what's his name? He's in a band'.

Musically, it's a hypnotic track based on Hannon's guitar arpeggios over a 6/4 time signature and employs a minimalistic chord sequence with a repeated movement between minor and major chords. This leads to a mantra-like effect that suggests an underlying drone and this is underlined by various throbbing and pulsing guitar-generated sounds. These sounds move subtly around the margins of the sound picture – a feature of this album on many of the tracks, and perhaps influenced by producer Nigel Godrich's previous work with Radiohead. There is also a subtle use of vibes to enhance this atmospheric song and some effective trombone slides on the coda from Stuart Bates that round off a mesmerising performance.

'Bad Ambassador' (Hannon)

The second single lifted from the album, it was surprising that this song didn't perform better than its lowly number 34 placing in May 2001. Here,

Hannon lists all the rock 'n' roll lifestyle behaviour he longs to get up to – such as buying expensive cars, riding Japanese motorbikes and indulging in pharmaceutical stimulation of the illegal kind. The title was inspired by a comment made by the band's manager about one of their road crew, calling him 'A bad ambassador for Ireland'.

It is one of the more orchestrated selections on this album and employs the Millennia Strings to add an arrangement that owes a debt to one of Hannon's ongoing influences: ELO. This is especially noticeable in the steep chromatic rise by the strings after the first line of the second chorus. Hannon adds some well-arranged lead guitar parts to the track, including a brief solo with plentiful string bends over a further chromatic sequence, this time slowly descending. It's a fairly chord-intensive affair and relatively complex for a short pop song.

'Perfect Lovesong' (Hannon)

The third single from the album and the most obvious choice for a pop single, it strives to imitate the perfect form of Brian Wilson and Tony Asher's 1966 Beach Boys hit 'God Only Knows'. Although not quite as perfect as that sublime beauty, 'Perfect Lovesong' does have a rather lovely structure. Lyrically, it's a song expressing Hannon's love for his wife Orla. The song claims to sport 'a divine Beatles bass line and a big old Beach Boys sound'. The verse is based on a cyclically descending chord sequence that does, indeed, echo 'God Only Knows', although the melody is quite different from that classic. The sound also recalls The Beach Boys with Wilson-style orchestration, catchy flute-like riffs (probably played on a keyboard) and some delicious reverb-tinged percussive touches that enhance the song's atmosphere. There is also a cello, played by Philip Sheppard, that underlines the descent of the later verses and adds to the Brian Wilson-like vibe of the song. All in all, it's a worthy tribute to the 1960s pop genius and deserved to fare better than its lowly peak of number 42 in the UK singles chart in November 2001.

'Note To Self' (Hannon)

In the most stripped-down arrangement yet, the two-chord guitar arpeggios are supported by a sauntering drum contribution from Miggy Barradas and an economical bass line from Bryan Mills. In the chorus, Hannon reflects on 'the heart of darkness' and being alone. A song of soul-searching honesty, he employs the days of the week to restate his assumptions, including: 'Heaven and hell do not exist'. The third verse brings an unexpected barrage of overdriven, thrashed electric guitar, sounding very grungy, as Hannon yells, 'What the fuck is happening?' – you get the feeling he is attempting to exorcise some personal demons with this track. It, again, features all sorts of throbbing and reverberant guitar-generated noises around the periphery of the sound picture, and some subtle orchestration from the Telefilmonic

Orchestra, with doorbell-like chimes accentuating the chord shifts towards the end. It is a less-than-happy sounding performance that is rather intense and, oddly, ends with a recording of two band members playing a game of ping-pong between recording takes!

'Lost Property' (Hannon)
At last, a song that deals with the seemingly endless stream of sundry items that mysteriously vanish from sight, never to be seen again. I'm sure everybody has their own personal lists of these mysteriously mislaid items that invariably disappear to some lost dimension. Neil Hannon has his own list of these and attempts to articulate the feeling of loss engendered by this curious phenomenon. The song was inspired by DC bassist Bryan Mills, who seems to have suffered a constant stream of vanishing objects. Hannon's own list includes the usual string of casualties: mobiles, chargers, asthma inhalers and the like, plus some more unusual items, including C-class narcotics, antibiotics, two tennis rackets, a blue Rizla packet and even a new sheepskin jacket.

The verse details the list of lost items, accompanied by some florid piano arpeggios, vacillating between minor and major chords. The verses lead into a second section with more exotic chords, including diminished sevenths and suspended ninths, which support a poignant vocal melody where Hannon sounds regretful in the extreme in his pining for these lost possessions. It is a profound reflection on the ephemeral nature of possession, in a world where, in reality, we never truly possess anything: the objects that we humans collect around us are, in a sense, just there to accompany us through a period of our existence, despite the sentimental meaning we attach to them. But the emotional climax of the song is a repeat of the second section, reoccurring towards the end, where Hannon's voice sounds truly distressed at the sense of loss he's suffering. This is until he has a dream where he passes through his lost sheepskin jacket and into that mysterious dimension where he finds his many lost items 'all piled up into the sky', resulting in 'tears of joy'. Subtly orchestrated, I personally find this track a strangely moving experience to listen to and it provides a definite highlight to the first half of the album.

'Eye Of The Needle' (Hannon)
A gentle, laid-back performance with a distinct ecclesiastical atmosphere, Hannon strums his acoustic guitar laconically in an arrangement built around piano, organ, trombone and bass – not forgetting a subtle contribution from a glockenspiel. It is an observational song about those wealthy churchgoers hoping, eventually, to thread themselves through the metaphorical 'eye of the needle', as reflected in the biblical quote from Matthew 19:24, attributed to Jesus Christ: 'It is easier for a camel to go through the eye of a needle than for a rich person to enter the Kingdom of God'. Hannon's lyric contrasts the

parked cars, which are 'shiny and German', as being 'at odds with the theme of the sermon'. It is also a song about those who strive to connect to a higher power through prayer but still feel no connection at all.

The coda employs a Bach-flavoured piano and organ passage that strongly recalls the sound of Procol Harum's late-1960s output, especially their 1967 number-one hit single 'A Whiter Shade Of Pale'. It makes for a peaceful end to the first half of *Regeneration*.

'Love What You Do' (Hannon)

This was the first single taken from the album and the highest charting of the trio of songs eventually released from *Regeneration*. It reached number 26 in March 2001, perhaps because it came out just before the album. It is a song that was written in the studio, following a period of band tension, and was inspired by a comment made to Hannon by producer Nigel Godrich: 'Love what you do or stop doing it'. Taken at a fair lick, this beat-driven offering moves along smartly and is the album's most positive song, reinforcing a 'Go for it' mantra. Amongst the advice dispensed by Hannon in the lyrics, are the sage suggestions to 'ditch your superstitions' and to 'lose your inhibitions'. It's a breezy performance without being one of the more galvanising tracks on the album. Likeable, but not a DC classic by any stretch of the imagination; it's one of those tracks that is hard to feel strongly about, one way or the other, but makes a bright enough start to the second half of *Regeneration*.

'Dumb It Down' (Hannon)

Next up is a song about society's constant but alarming exponential drift towards the lowest common denominator, especially where the media is concerned. As Hannon describes it: 'It's about how the media think the public is stupid', as everything seems to be constantly 'dumbed down', with quality (and truth) often taking a back seat. People's attention spans are encouraged to shrink and the population is fed a constant stream of unedifying jargon and images via newspapers, TV and the internet.

Musically, this mid-paced track is guitar-driven, with a verse using variations on a minor chord and a see-sawing vocal melody, while the chorus of 'Down and down and down we go' employs a suitably descending chord sequence. By the last chorus, Hannon sounds in despair, as the track ends with his desperate plea – 'Is there anybody listening?'

'Mastermind' (Hannon)

The highest quality song on the second half of the album, 'Mastermind' sounds as if Hannon has been listening to 'Celluloid Heroes'-era Ray Davies, as even his vocal displays the fragility and melancholia that were the hallmark of The Kinks' chief songwriter. It's a chord-intensive song with a delicious sequence and a beguiling tune. The key lines of the song look for affirmation that the protagonist is 'normal' and 'sane'. It started life as a country song before it was rearranged once producer Nigel Godrich took over the reins for the recording sessions.

It is based on a matrix of piano arpeggios with some nice orchestration, which enhances its expressive melody. By the end of the song, Hannon has amended the chorus chant to ask just who is normal and who is sane. A reasonable question to ponder, in my view.

Trivia note: Incidentally, Neil Hannon has appeared several times on the BBC TV quiz show *Celebrity Mastermind*, and on the 3 January 2012 episode, he was the winner of the coveted trophy – his chosen specialist subject was the TV show, *Frasier*. He also re-appeared in the black chair on an episode aired on 28 December 2020, with the specialist subject this time being his beloved *Merchant Ivory* adaptations of EM Forster novels – although James Haskell ended up winning the trophy on that occasion.

'Regeneration' (Hannon)

The second half of the album's title track is probably the closest Hannon ever came to a hard rock styling, although the song gets through quite a number of different chords in its short duration. The most memorable part of the arrangement is the hard-rock riff that appears in the second half of the song – a riff that would feel quite at home on a heavy rock album.

Lyrically, it is a song about rebirth and creativity, quite literally in the verse after the middle eight, when Hannon sings 'X plus Y equals new life' in reference to chromosomes. The song also acts as a metaphor for Hannon's new, back-to-basics musical thrust – a reinvention of The Divine Comedy for the new century. In many ways, it's one of the less interesting tracks presented here, but in the context of the album, it works as a contrast piece to the more sophisticated songs presented elsewhere.

'The Beauty Regime' (Hannon)

Taking its title from a lifestyle magazine that Hannon allegedly read whilst sitting on a toilet, the lyrical thrust of the song is to reject advice in such publications as to how you should look, act or what you should wear; instead, just be yourself. Moving at a slow tempo in triple time, it sports a captivating melody over an impressive chord sequence and another of Hannon's fragile vocals that, not for the first time on this album, recall Ray Davies in more sensitive mode. The tune is a real grower and it seeps into the subconscious after several listens. It makes for a supremely laid-back and relaxing end to the album.

Additional Material

'Soul Trader' (Hannon)

Many of Neil Hannon's songs from this period sound as if they are channelling Ray Davies and this is yet another example where his vocal style sounds close to that of The Kinks' redoubtable frontman, especially on the choruses, where it modulates upward. It's a song that chugs along at a medium tempo, with a somewhat oblique lyric about the kind of character that people just can't say no to. It is something of a minor track by DC standards, but chunters along agreeably and it does have its own sense of charm. There is an instrumental section where an organ sticks to the vocal melody line and a neat turnaround at the end. It was originally released on the 'Love What You Do' CD1 single on 26 February 2001.

'You' (Hannon)

Sounding as if it could have come from the 1990 DC debut album *Fanfare For The Comic Muse*, this is the most REM-influenced song since those early days. It's an engaging little love song, driven by an acoustic rhythm guitar along with electric guitar arpeggios over some nifty rhythmic punctuation, followed by a Byrds-flavoured descending arpeggio. Along with its tuneful harmonised chorus, this gives the song a lovely seamless flow. It's a very 'up' sounding song, and lyrically, it is probably a love note to Hannon's wife Orla. It first appeared along with 'Soul Trader' on the 'Love What You Do' CD1 single (see previous entry).

'Edward The Confessor' (Hannon)

A song of unabashed apology, this is an anthem for all of us who constantly feel that we need to say 'sorry'. It has a slow, dirge-like ambience that is darkly fascinating and it seems it may be Hannon himself who's apologising, as Edward is his real first name. We can, therefore, assume that this is most likely a personal song, rather than a character-driven one. He strums along diffidently on his acoustic guitar, as he lists his perceived faults in the verse and begs forgiveness in the 'I'm so sorry' choruses, where piano chords enter. The drums keep a steady beat in the background, and later, some discreet vibes join in. It's definitely not a feel-good song, but it does sound sincere and from the heart. The track was first released on the 'Bad Ambassador' CD1 single on 14 May 2001. Edward the Confessor was also, of course, the last in a line of Anglo-Saxon kings from the House of Wessex prior to the Norman invasion of 1066.

'U.S.E' (Hannon)

The UK was much more a part of Europe when this song was written – before the word 'Brexit' had even been coined. In its chorus, Hannon asks the question, 'Is you in, or is you ain't?' – U.S.E. standing for the United States of Europe. The three verses take turns to parody characteristics of the Germans, French and Italians, with much humour and tongue firmly in cheek. Hannon ponders on fast cars on German autobahns, French strikes and those 'so damned cool' Italians 'With a brand new government every day'. It's a track possessing a muscular chug via Hannon's storming barrel-house piano, as well as a somewhat springy-sounding guitar with sitar-like overtones.

'Les Jours Tristes' (Tiersen, Hannon)

This collaboration with French Breton composer Yann Tiersen is one of the more interesting tracks tucked away as single B-sides. Neil Hannon's vocal contribution was recorded at The Dairy in Brixton, London, in 2000 and the song was featured on Tiersen's 2001 album *L'Absente*. The Breton composer's accordion pumps along the action to a triple-time rhythm set against a piano/guitar backing. The strong Breton flavour of the music is all-pervading and evinces a sad/happy kind of vibe. The arrangement starts more sparsely but builds up quite a head of steam, as orchestral tones are gradually introduced, until, towards the end, it seems as if there is a veritable symphony going on behind Hannon's earnest vocals. It's a track that will reward repeated listens, as it builds a rich orchestral swirl under the relentless, pumping rhythm thanks to the 45-piece, Synaxis, Vienne Vallee du Rhone Ensemble.

Hannon's lyrics reflect on the unrelenting hardship encountered in facing the brickbats that life throws our way, sometimes making it difficult to plough on with our daily lives. But as he asserts in the lyric, 'It's hard, but you know it's worth the fight'. It's a song of fortitude, but also of encouragement and is uplifting for that reason. The French title *Les Jours Tristes* translates into English as 'the sad days'. It featured on the DC single 'Perfect Lovesong' CD1, released on 29 October 2001.

'Thinking The Unthinkable' (Hannon)

Originally released on the single 'Perfect Lovesong' CD2, along with a cover of Bryan Ferry's 'Oh Yeah', this song finds Neil Hannon in doubtful mode, as he cogitates on a series of potential disasters and doom-laden maybes in the verses and relates these to a more personal feeling of disquiet in the choruses.

The foreboding in the lyrics is reflected in the music, which carries a powerful underlying feeling of uneasiness. The arrangement is underpinned by Hannon's electric piano and rhythm guitar playing, communicating an indie vibe. After the choruses, in which he laments doubtfully, 'I've started to wonder, what a terrible blunder I've made', he adds some rather thin-sounding slide guitar licks, and, later in the track, a short slide solo. There is a middle eight thrown in, where he reasons, 'I'm not superhuman', as he realises, 'All I can do is try'. Nevertheless, he really shouldn't be so hard on himself considering the peerless canon of work he has bequeathed the world – but then again, we all have our moments of self-doubt.

Above: Neil Hannon played two solo gigs at El Rey Theatre, Los Angeles on 27 and 28 March 2002, supporting Ben Folds. (*Alamy*)

Left: The Divine Comedy's 1990 debut album, *Fanfare For The Comic Muse* found Neil Hannon firmly under the spell of REM. (*Setanta Records*)

Right: The second DC album, *Liberation* initiated 1990s chamber-pop and was on another artistic level from the 1990 debut album. (*Setanta Records*)

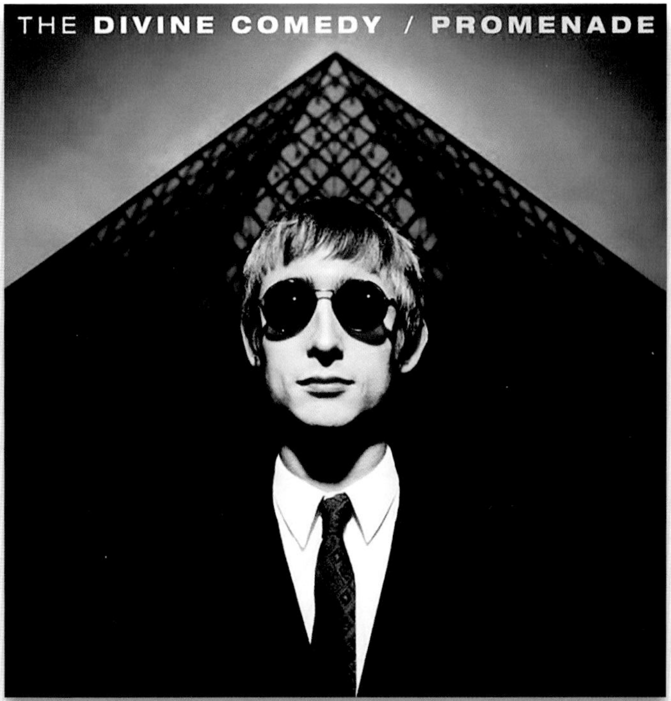

Right: The third DC album, *Promenade* marked an early milestone in 1994 and remains a firm favourite with fans. (*Setanta Records*)

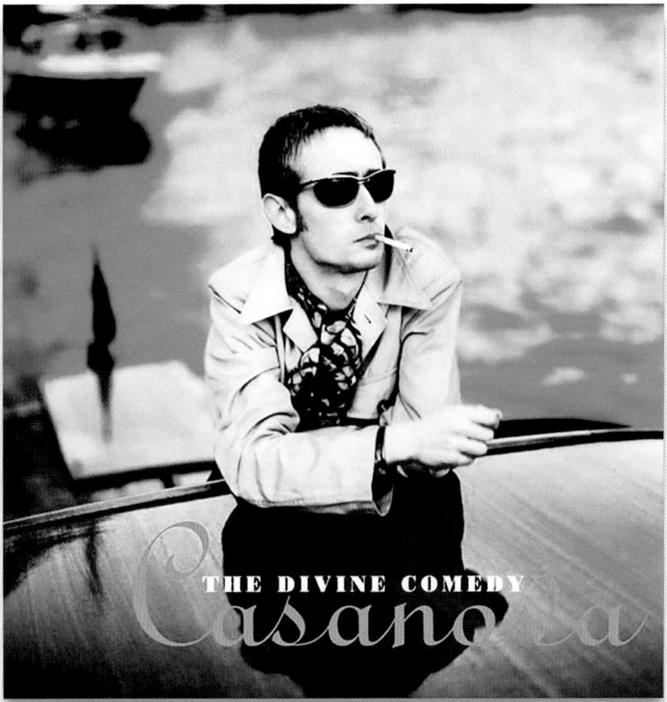

Left: Britpop influences dominated on the fourth DC album *Casanova*, resulting in three hit singles. (*Setanta Records*)

Left: Recorded live, *A Short Album About Love* was the best-selling DC album yet, gaining a silver disc in 1997. (*Setanta Records*)

Right: Released in 1998, *Fin De Siecle* displayed a vaunting ambition and three more hits, including a number eight in 'National Express'. (*Setanta Records*)

Right: *Regeneration* ushered in a new era for Neil Hannon in 2001, with its back-to-basics approach. (*Parlophone Records*)

Left: Ornate orchestration made a stunning return on the eighth DC studio album *Absent Friends* in 2004. (*Parlophone Records*)

Left: The single 'Becoming More Like Alfie', released on 12 August 1996, was the second DC hit single of the year.

Right: Neil Hannon turns his camera on the camera! Another video still from 'Becoming More Like Alfie'.

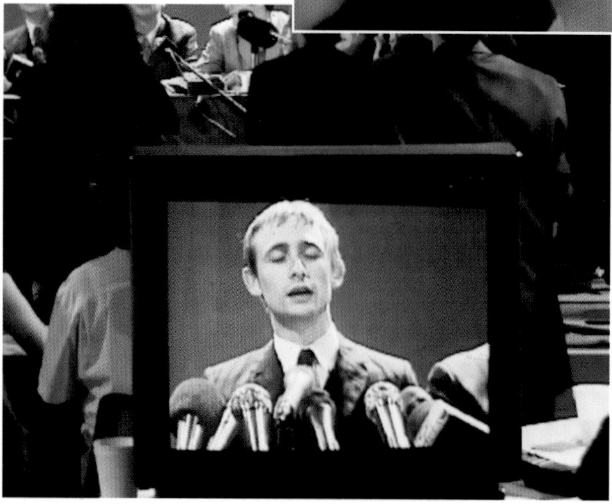

Left: 'The Certainty Of Chance' made for an unusual single release on 9 November 1998, accompanied by its promo video.

Right: 'Love What You Do' was the first single release from the *Regeneration* album and another Top-30 UK hit.

Left: Neil Hannon emotes in another video still from the 'Love What You Do' promo.

Right: The 'Bad Ambassador' video promoted this second single from *Regeneration*. It was a number 34 UK hit in May 2001.

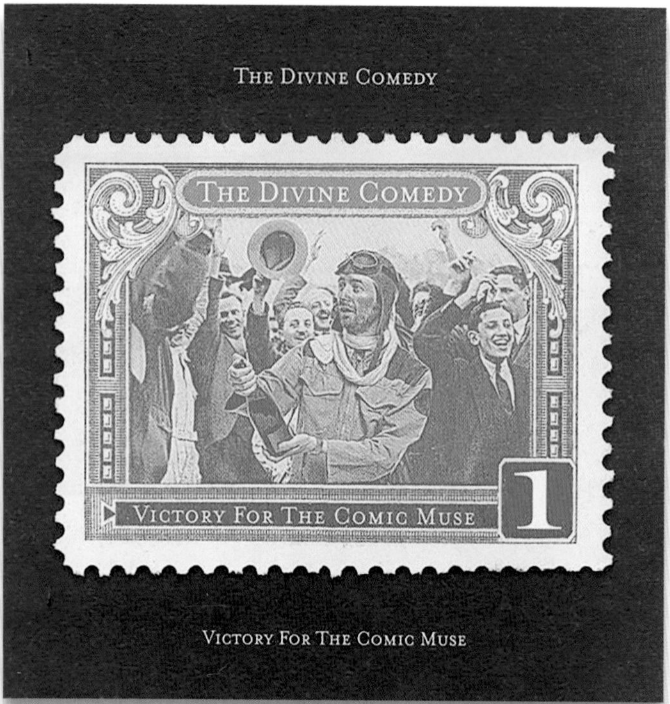

Left: A noble attempt at recording live in the studio on analogue equipment, *Victory For The Comic Muse* was released in 2006. (*Parlophone Records*)

Right: In 2009, Neil Hannon and Thomas Walsh unveiled the world's first 'cricket-pop' album: *The Duckworth Lewis Method*. (*Divine Comedy Records*)

Right: The piano-based 2010 album *Bang Goes The Knighthood* is packed with sharply observed character sketches. (*Divine Comedy Records*)

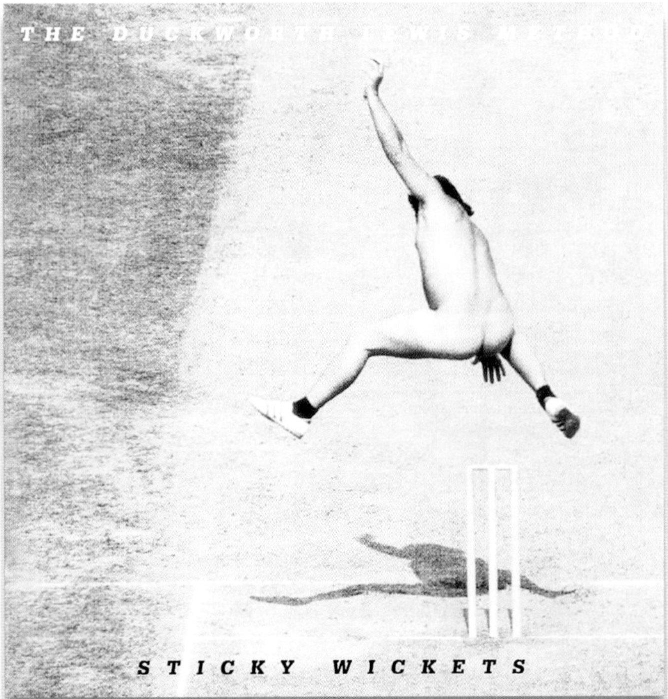

Left: The Duckworth Lewis Method returned in 2013 with more songs about cricket on *Sticky Wickets*. (*Divine Comedy Records*)

Left: The DLM 2013 single 'It's Just Not Cricket' was accompanied by an amusing promo video featuring the pair.

Right: Lewis (Neil Hannon, left) and Duckworth (Thomas Walsh, right) prop up the bar in the 'It's Just Not Cricket' video.

Left: Neil Hannon spears a tasty snack with his rapier in the video for 'How Can You Leave Me On My Own'.

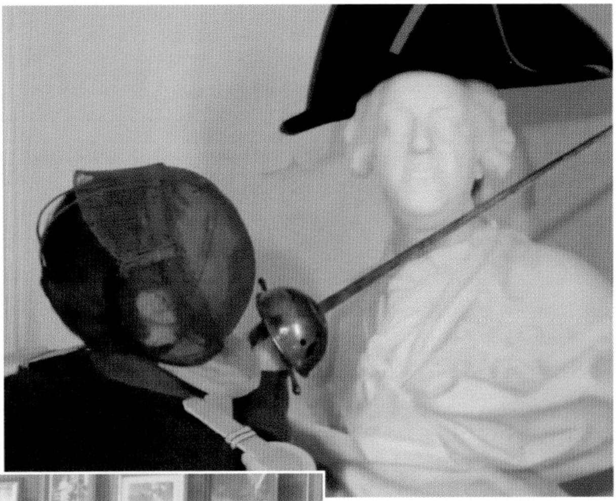

Right: More fencing antics from Hannon during the 'How Can You Leave Me On My Own' video.

Left: A still from the 2019 'Norman And Norma' video, promoting the first single release from the *Office Politics* album.

Right: Released as a 7" single in October 2019, this is a still from the video promoting 'Infernal Machines'.

Above: Neil Hannon at London's Rock Garden, with the *Fanfare* incarnation of The Divine Comedy, on 9 August 1990. (*Guy Van Steene, indiethroughthelookingglass.com*)

Above: The Divine Comedy in Munich, 21 February 1996, on a short tour supporting Supergrass. (*Alamy*)

Above: Neil Hannon and guitarist Tosh Flood performing on the *Office Politics* tour in 2019. (*Bernie McAllister*)

Left: The superbly orchestrated *Foreverland* restored The Divine Comedy to the Top Ten in 2016. (*Divine Comedy Records*)

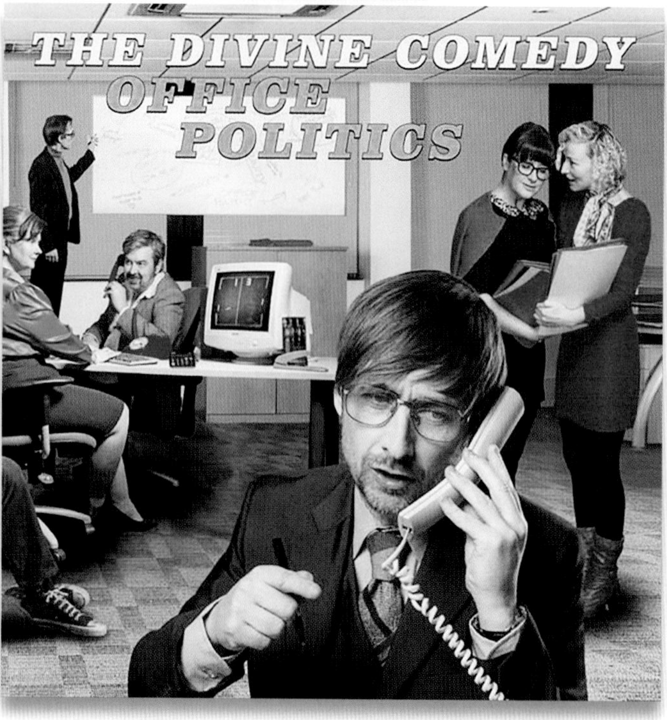

Right: The eclectic mix of songs on the 2019 DC album *Office Politics* explored the world of work and the rise of machines. (*Divine Comedy Records*)

Right: *A Secret History* is a superb 'Best of' compilation, closing the Setanta years in style in 1999. (*Setanta Records*)

Left: *Charmed Life* was a Top Five hit for The Divine Comedy in 2022, including the all-new *Super Extra Bonus Album*. (*Divine Comedy Records*)

Left: 'The Best Mistakes' was an excellent new song from *Charmed Life*, accompanied by a charming video. (*Divine Comedy Records*)

Right: A dramatic blue shot of Neil Hannon in the promo video for 'The Best Mistakes'.

Left: Neil Hannon reflecting on life in the promo video for 'The Best Mistakes'.

Absent Friends (2004)

Personnel:
Neil Hannon: vocals, guitar, keyboards, bass
Joby Talbot: plucked piano ('Freedom Road'), string arrangements, conducting
Rob Farrer: percussion
Miggy Barradas: drums ('Sticks & Stones', 'Come Home Billy Bird', 'The Happy Goth', 'Charmed Life')
Simon Little: double bass ('The Happy Goth')
Crispin Robinson: congas ('Come Home Billy Bird', 'The Happy Goth')
Lauren Laverne: vocals ('Come Home Billy Bird')
Yann Tiersen: accordion ('Sticks & Stones')
Matt Gunner: horn ('Freedom Road')
Nick Cartledge: flute solo ('The Happy Goth')
Everton Nelson: Millennia Strings – Leader, violin solo ('Laika's Theme')
Charles Mutter, Warren Zielinski, Cath Haggo, Natalia Bonner, Giles Broadbent, Rik Koster, Matthew Scrivener, Alison Dods, Darragh Morgan, Richard George, Steve Hussey, Tim Myall, Helena Wood, John Smart, Maya Bickell, Jenny Sacha, Vince Greene, Adrian Smith, Louise Hogan, Reiad Chibab, Dan Cornford, Jay Craig, Chris Worsey, Ian Burdge, Nick Holland, Chris Fish, Lucy Shaw, Bev Jones, Lucy Wakeford, Dan Newell, Tim Rees-Roberts, James Spaddy Adams, Mike Kearsy, Matt Gunner, Simon Morgan, Nick Cartledge, Dom Kelly, Jo Cackett, Gareth Newman, Chris Richards: Millennia Strings (fixed by Jonathan Brigden)
Recorded at RAK, Abbey Road, Intimate and Konk Studios, London between May 2002 and September 2003
Mixed at Mayfair Studios, London by Nigel Godrich, assisted by Dan Grech-Marguerat
Engineer: Guy Massey, assisted by Raj Das and Chris Bolster
Producer: Neil Hannon
Record label: Parlophone
Released: 29 March 2004
Highest UK chart position: 23

Following the release of *Regeneration*, the seven-piece Divine Comedy undertook an intensive period of gigging throughout 2001, both in the UK and Europe. Interestingly, Neil Hannon paid homage to one of his earliest, enduring influences when he narrated *Mr. Blue Sky – The Jeff Lynne Story* on BBC Radio 2, a two-part programme broadcast on the 2 and 9 June that year. The gigging continued into the autumn, until, on 23 October, it was announced that the current line-up of the band would be breaking up and a proposed album for 2002 would not go ahead. Instead, Hannon continued to compose new material through the next two years, as he was still signed to Parlophone Records. The band did, however, complete two final tours in late 2001 to support the single 'Perfect Lovesong'.

On 19 December, Neil Hannon became a father when his daughter Willow Mary Enn Hannon was born, and this would strongly influence his writing for the next DC album, which he would dedicate to her. In February 2002, a trio version of The Divine Comedy, consisting of Neil Hannon, Ivor Talbot and Rob Farrer, undertook a short US tour. As this moved into March, Hannon played solo support on a Ben Folds tour that crisscrossed the States, piling in 25 dates before the end of the month. By May, he initiated the first sessions for *Absent Friends* at Konk Studios, London, with Guy Massey assisting with the recording. He then returned to the US in June for another 15-date tour supporting Ben Folds, all the while writing new material to be recorded on his return to the UK. On 10 July, an expanded line-up of The Divine Comedy, with a line-up of Hannon, Ivor Talbot, Rob Farrer, Stuart 'Pinkie' Bates and double-bassist Simon Little, played support to David Bowie at the Move Festival in Manchester. Further sessions for the new album took place at Intimate Studios, London in October, following an Irish tour with Ben Folds, who joined The Divine Comedy for their encore numbers. Some interesting cover versions were performed, including George Michael's 'Careless Whisper', Burt Bacharach's 'Raindrops Keep Falling On My Head' and The Flaming Lips' 'Race For The Prize'. Further DC American dates filled the remainder of 2002.

By July 2003, Hannon had returned to RAK Studios in London, where Joby Talbot, again, became involved, assisting on string arrangements for the new album, followed by a move to Abbey Road in August to record the orchestral parts. In October, Hannon first met up with Thomas Walsh from the band Pugwash and he would eventually go on to record a brace of albums with Walsh from 2009 onwards, billed as The Duckworth-Lewis Method.

The artwork for *Absent Friends* reverted to a portrait of Neil Hannon on its cover, this time draped across a chaise lounge and looking to be in deep contemplation – an image that perfectly reflected this richly orchestrated and mindful collection of compositions. On its release on 29 March 2004, there were the usual mixed reviews from the media, the most favourable of which appeared in *The Word*, who reckoned the album was 'Cerebral, heartfelt and delicately constructed', also stating that 'The old warmth of early Divine Comedy is back in style'. Meanwhile, *The Fly* called *Absent Friends* 'Stately, intelligent and deeply moving'. I would personally concur with these views, as a more mature Neil Hannon, now in his early 30s, managed a perfect blend of his influences, the most obvious of which were Scott Walker, Michael Nyman and Jacques Brel (he had recently recorded a cover of Brel's 'Jackie' for a compilation album of Brel covers called *Next*, released in late 2003).

The first single from the album sessions, 'Come Home Billy Bird', was released on 22 March 2004 and hit the UK singles chart in April, peaking at number 25. The *Absent Friends* album followed on 29 March and spent a month on the UK album chart, reaching number 23. The title track became the second single released from the album, but only managed a rather lowly number 38 in June. *Absent Friends* was an album that certainly deserved more commercial success than it achieved, but, in truth, the days of Top 20 placings for DC albums seemed to have passed (for a while). However,

Hannon's dedicated fan base always ensured that DC albums made a chart showing on initial sales, even if the chart runs were briefer these days. August saw the release of *The Bavarian EP*, a duo of live tracks from the 2004 tour ('No-one Knows' – a cover of the Queens Of The Stone Age song from their 2002 album *Music For The Deaf* – and the old DC classic 'Three Sisters'), plus an acoustic demo of the *Absent Friends* album track 'Our Mutual Friend'.

'Absent Friends' (Hannon)

It's clear from the title track alone that Neil Hannon had been listening to the 'Spaghetti Western' soundtracks of Ennio Morricone, with a return to the galloping rhythm previously employed on several classic DC songs. This rhythm, combined with a big orchestral string and brass arrangement, gives this track its distinctive 'Wild West' feel, reinforced in the latter part of the song by a brief Mexicali trumpet solo and a string arrangement that owes a lot to Jerome Moross' film theme for the 1958 Western *The Big Country*. This theme had also previously been borrowed by progressive rock band Yes on their 1970 album *Time And A Word*, as part of their cover of Richie Havens' 'No Opportunity Necessary, No Experience Needed'.

Lyrically, 'Absent Friends' commemorates a handful of characters from the last 150 years, beginning with actress Jean Seberg, who committed suicide in September 1979. An influence on Neil Hannon from early on in his career, a sample of her iconic appearance in the 1960 film *Breathless* had been used on the DC track 'When The Lights Go Out All Over Europe' from the 1994 album *Promenade*.

The next verse pays tribute to 'Woodbine Willie', otherwise known as Geoffrey Studdert Kennedy: an Anglican Priest and poet who, during the First World War, obtained his nickname by handing out Woodbine cigarettes to the troops he was caring for in the trenches.

Between the 'Woodbine Willie' verse and the next one, which is dedicated to actor Steve McQueen, the key modulates up a tone, accompanied by a revving sound effect, presumably representing the stolen motorcycle that McQueen used in his performance as Virgil Hilts, 'The Cooler King' in the 1963 film *The Great Escape*. In the film, he jumps the barbed-wire fences on this stolen motorcycle in an attempt to escape from German POW camp *Stalag Luft III*, but unfortunately, German soldiers shoot out one of his tyres and he is recaptured.

An unusual tribute to pioneering canine Laika makes up the next verse, the first of two eulogies to her on this album. Laika was the first living creature to go into space, when the Soviet Union launched her into orbit in Sputnik 2 on 3 November 1957. Callously, there were no plans to retrieve her from orbit (a means of achieving a safe return to Earth had not yet evolved in 1957). A stray mongrel picked up from the streets of Moscow, Laika is commemorated on the *Monument To The Conquerors Of Space* obelisk, erected in Moscow in 1964.

The final verse is dedicated to Irish writer Oscar Wilde, a former pupil of Hannon's childhood educational establishment, Portora Royal School in Enniskillen. In the song, Hannon laments: 'They drove poor Oscar to his grave'. The last verse of the song, like the first, invites us to raise a toast to these and other 'Absent Friends', as over the galloping strings, Hannon croons fetchingly: 'Happy days, we thought that they would never end – but they always end'. The Western ambience of the music carries right through to the end of the song. A single strike upon a tubular bell brings this DC classic to a close.

'Sticks & Stones' (Hannon)

With an unremittingly stark arrangement of staccato cello and violin strokes propelling it, the verses shift across two minor chords, backing a lugubrious Hannon vocal. Yann Tiersen's cascading accordion lines decorate this intense musical landscape from the second verse onwards, and the whole thing strongly recalls the style of Hannon's hero, Scott Walker. The feel of this track nods back to the *Promenade* album in its austere ambience. It's a song about how unkind words can often wound more deeply than physical abuse. Hannon ponders on a relationship, comparing the couple's compatibility to 'the molar and the drill', concluding that 'flesh is weak' but that 'the ego's weaker still'. After two verses, the chorus arrives, moving momentarily into a major key for a reverse twist on a well-known saying: 'sticks and stones may break my bones', with a conclusion that unkind words can be just as hurtful. As the track progresses, the string arrangement builds into an orchestral coda, evincing an extravagant grandiosity, complete with violins, cello and a gong.

'Leaving Today' (Hannon)

The recent birth of his daughter Willow seems to have brought forth a rash of more personal songs from Neil Hannon in the preparation for this album, this being one of them. Many of the songs on *Absent Friends* were written during his crowded US touring schedule, where he was crisscrossing the States for much of 2002, while Willow was in her first year. This emotionally charged song reflects on the fact that he has to leave for extended periods of touring, forsaking his wife and young baby, left alone at home. Heart-wrenchingly sentimental in tone, his superb talent as a wordsmith ensures that maudlin territory is avoided. Hannon's poetically observational description of even the simple act of waking up and rousing himself at some unearthly hour paints a riveting picture. The line, 'No light from yonder window breaks', is a nod to Shakespeare's *Romeo & Juliet*, and a mention of the intrusive sound of an alarm clock underscores the wrench he feels at having to leave his family. But duty calls and a living must be earned. After peeping around the nursery door and then bidding a fond farewell to his wife, the inevitable taxi arrives to transport him to the airport and yet another tour across the North American continent.

The music perfectly reflects Hannon's state of mind, as the song opens with drifting four-note arpeggios that tonally sound halfway between a harp and a guitar. As the subtle orchestration builds in the background, Hannon's tormented voice strongly brings to mind Scott Walker and the track sounds uncannily in the style of Walker's iconic first four solo albums from the late 1960s. It almost feels as if the song is in stasis, such is the minimal forward momentum of this curiously floating creation. The harmonically rich chord progression lends the song a feeling of deep sadness, and in an inspired final verse, Hannon evokes raindrops running down the taxi windows as representing fading dreams. 'They blur the street lamps as we pass', he sings, as the song ends unresolved on an Amb6 chord, concluding a masterful piece of songwriting.

'Come Home Billy Bird' (Hannon)

The first single released from the album and a Top 30 UK hit, it is essentially the tale of a hung-over international business traveller attempting to fly home in time for his son's big football game. Opening with an orchestral prelude, we're soon into a lightly cantering tempo, driven by a rhythmic guitar playing simple major chords. There are some striking reverb effects on Miggy Barradas' snare drum beat as the track progresses, enhancing the rhythm of the track. The catchy chorus is sung by Lauren Laverne and contrasts nicely with the Hannon-sung verses. A descending 12-string electric guitar solo breaks up the action halfway through the song, perhaps representing the descent of the aircraft that William Bird is heading home in. Again, Hannon's preoccupation with a father figure being away from home surfaces in this tale of a frequently absent parent, fitting in snugly with the concept of absence explored on this album. Mr. William Bird will make another lyrical appearance 15 years down the line when he reappears in the song 'Office Politics' and then disappears in the song "Opportunity' Knox' – both from the 2019 DC album *Office Politics*.

'My Imaginary Friend' (Hannon)

This cute, light-hearted song examines that curious childhood phenomenon of the 'imaginary friend'. In our early years, most of us have had one of these: mine was a mouse called Midge! This particular lad has a make-believe pal called Benjamin and his obsession with this character appears to be driving his parents 'round the bend'. Hannon's clever use of language never fails to amuse and you are unlikely to come across many other pop songs that rhyme 'mobile library' with 'peripatetically'. Sadly, as we mature, our imaginary friends invariably vanish – in this case, precipitated by a game of hide-and-seek – leaving the enigmatic Benjamin 'up the creek' and 'never to be seen again' as he inevitably disappears, along with childhood at the onset of adolescence. The heart-warming thing here is that our maturing youngster has never forgotten his imaginary friend – much like I've never forgotten Midge the mouse!

The musical accompaniment is as charming as the song's lyrics, as guitar chords play on the offbeat at a briskly strolling tempo and a plucked banjo provides replies between the vocals. A piano becomes prominent from the second verse onwards. The middle section of the song sees Hannon cleverly singing low-toned, Mike Love-style, Beach Boys' backing vocals on the beat, while a further vocal line spells out the song title with two letters to the bar. All in all, this is a pleasantly amusing diversion amongst some of the more intense tracks of this album.

'The Wreck Of The Beautiful' (Hannon)

The intro of this track comes over as something of a sound experiment. It's an eerily atmospheric, floating, tuned percussion passage, sonically similar to the tone of tuned water bottles, crossed with a sound akin to a submerged marimba – overall, it generates a ghostly ambience. Along with what sounds like slowly plucked harp arpeggios (but possibly played on a guitar), it uncannily brings to mind the vision of murky ocean depths, as the track drifts gently forward with a touch of dissonance in the mix. This effect is perfect for a song that is ostensibly about an old ship that has seen better days and is about to be decommissioned and taken to the breakers' yard. The whole song floats along atmospherically and the lyrics tell the tale of 'The Beautiful', a vessel that was state-of-the-art when launched in 1970, but, in the fullness of time, became rusted by sea salt. A discordant keyboard line enters under the vocals, adding to the eerie feeling on display.

The minor key choruses are particularly haunting, as a reverb-drenched voice, sounding amazingly like ELO's Jeff Lynne, sings, 'I thought I heard her call', followed by a deeper reply vocal: 'Maybe I heard nothing at all'. Here, Hannon has uncannily tapped into Jeff Lynne's vocal sound (always one of his prime influences). This line really nails the vocal feel that Lynne achieved back in the 1970s on tracks like 'Waterfall' from *Face The Music* (1975) and 'Can't Get It Out Of My Head' from *Eldorado* (1974).

After the first chorus and a return of the ambient intro passage, the orchestration on the second verse becomes more dramatic and the music builds to a crescendo, as Hannon hears the aforementioned ship's 'voice' call and sees mountainous waves five miles high! It's all pure melodrama, but somehow carries an emotional intensity that permeates so much of this extraordinary album. That eerily lovely chorus arrives once more before the coda moves to a deep-toned, horn-like riff, which evokes a ship moving through a fog bank as the music fades.

It is interesting that Hannon picked 1970 as the launch year of 'The Beautiful' in this song, as it was also the year of his own birth – it's always tempting to read other meanings into Hannon's songs and wonder whether this nautical tale was maybe meant as an allegory of some kind. Listen and decide for yourself.

'Our Mutual Friend' (Hannon)

In many ways, the masterpiece of the album, this is a song that truly harks back to Hannon's 'baroque period' of 1993/1994. It boasts a stunning orchestral arrangement for three violins, a cello, a trumpet, two French horns, three tubas, a clarinet, two bassoons, cor anglais, a flute, a harp, percussion and piano. The arrangement has a similarly stark feel to that employed on the track 'Sticks & Stones', but here, the intensity is racked up a fair few notches more, once the music is combined with Hannon's lyrics. These relate an intense tale of falling for a girl, who is introduced by a mutual friend. Moving on from pub to nightclub, they all end up going back to the friend's place, worse the wear with drink. As this scenario progresses, the couple get to know each other by playing 'old 45s' together – they try to dance but end up tottering and eventually kissing. However, due to excessive inebriation, they eventually fall unconscious.

Our protagonist awakes some time later, alone ('but for a headache'), and staggers out in search of the bathroom but instead finds the new girl of his dreams 'wrapped around another lover' (the mutual friend of the title). This story takes on a riveting intensity due to the song's inspired arrangement. Such is the tension engendered by this performance, it's hard to believe this song isn't autobiographical.

There are many brilliant musical touches to savour: the virtuosity of the sawing strings, the plaintive cor anglais lines between the intensity of the verses and the clever way the strings emphasise the feeling of waking with a hangover in the verse. This is where the protagonist awakes from his drunken stupor – a vision brought to life by the long, slightly dissonant-sounding violin and cello strokes across each bar. This was a track that appealed to fans of both the earlier and later periods of The Divine Comedy's career and is regarded as a DC classic by most fans. At one point, Hannon refers to a song that the protagonist and his prospective girlfriend sang together, whilst they were spinning the 'old 45s', as a song that he can't sing anymore. This song was later revealed to be 'The Sun Ain't Gonna Shine Anymore' – a hit for The Walker Brothers in 1965. In various live performances, Hannon inserts this information back into the lyrics, making 'Our Mutual Friend' feel like it's really coming from the heart.

'The Happy Goth' (Hannon)

With its sad/happy duality, this is a track that switches moods and tempos swiftly as it proceeds. It is addressing a beautiful young girl who pursues the 'Goth' lifestyle and ploughs her own lonely furrow, seeming to be content with her own company for a good deal of the time. In these opening verses, Hannon enquires tenderly of her, 'Is everything alright?'. The initial verse opens with a B minor guitar arpeggio, before moving to a lightly skipping Gm7, with several twists and turns of tempo, before finally firming up for a catchy, lightly swinging B minor chorus. This chorus has an almost happy-go-lucky feel, enhanced by Simon Little's double bass contribution. Its happier feel makes an effective contrast with the more poignant initial variations of the opening verses. It has a gentle melody, which is memorable and extremely hummable. In this chorus, Hannon compares the whiteness of her face to 'the snows of Hoth', in reference to the snowy planet from the *Star Wars* film franchise.

In the third verse, an imaginary conversation occurs between the Goth girl and her parents, attempting to reassure them and allay their fears for her, but alas, no conversation of this kind is likely to take place in reality, as she keeps things to herself, taking a different path in search of an identity. The song moves towards its close with two more of those deliciously catchy choruses, with what sounds like a bass saxophone providing the bottom end, imparting an almost jaunty swing to proceedings. Sandwiched between the last two choruses is an orchestral instrumental over the chorus chords, which emphasises the song's gorgeous melody. The last chorus ends unresolved on F# minor, perhaps reflecting the Goth girl's inner turmoil. This makes way for an ingenious ending, as Crispin Robinson's tasteful conga playing underpins an ever-ascending flute solo by Nick Cartledge. The flute spirals upwards with lightning runs and trills, providing an enthralling close to this enchanting song.

'Freedom Road' (Hannon)

This song is a perfect example of how to write something special using very few chords. Hannon picks a slow arpeggio on guitar, moving to-and-fro across an AMaj9 chord – the sound of which evokes time slowly ticking by. For the lyrics, he employs a deeper tone than usual, sounding remarkably like Johnny Cash. He relates the story of a trucker traversing the Interstate-19 highway, which runs from just short of the Mexican border, northwards towards Tucson, Arizona. During the course of the song, the trucker appears to undergo some kind of spiritual awakening while out on the road. The song opens early one morning with said trucker lamenting that he will soon have to put up with 'The whole world and his Uncle Joe' congesting his 'Freedom Road'. By verse four, he starts to get reflective and attempts to mentally reconcile his younger self's vision of the 'Freedom Road' with reality, yearning to 'shed this heavy load'.

Up to this point, the music has resolutely remained on just one chord, enhanced by Matt Gunner's long horn lines – that chord being the aforementioned AMaj9. Here, Hannon shows uncanny skill and perfect timing; following the line where the trucker laments about his 'heavy load', the sudden chord change to F feels like a revelation after so long building over just one chord. Few songwriters show this instinctive sense of timing – that of picking the precise moment to say *now*.

By verse five, we return to the slowly picked AMaj9 chord and our protagonist is clearly in some sort of crisis. Waxing eloquently on the power of the landscape, as observed throughout his travels, he describes mighty lightning storms, huge American wheat fields and a sunrise over the lakes, and, on which his comment is: 'And that shit takes my breath away'. This line sees a further effective return to an F chord again. Knowing that his truck stop friends would never understand his newly burgeoning sensitivity, a final return to the AMaj9 chord finds our trucker parking up his rig and just walking away. This song was most likely written by Hannon on those seemingly endless tours of the States in 2002, and 'Freedom Road' remains one of the most American-sounding examples of DC music.

'Laika's Theme' (Hannon)

This instrumental is the second tribute on the album to the Soviet space dog Laika, the sole living occupant of the satellite Sputnik 2, back in 1957. It's a story I was familiar with as a young kid, growing up through the 1960s, as I was a complete space nut, and, at the time, knew the details of every American and Soviet space mission undertaken. Laika's story has always both touched and horrified me, as she was doomed to a one-way trip from the moment of lift-off. She died after four days when the ventilation system failed (although this only came to light later; at the time, the Soviets claimed Laika was alive for six days and then put to sleep humanely).

This spacey-sounding instrumental perfectly evokes the weightlessness that would've been experienced by Laika in Earth orbit and it carries a poignant sadness in its interweaving melodies that float, as if in the void. It is also surpassingly beautiful in tone, with crystalline arpeggios, ambient keyboard sounds and violin by Millennia Strings' leader Everton Nelson, well integrated into the mix of spaced-out keyboard lines. Neil Hannon must have been as touched and saddened as I was by Laika's story, him being such a dog-lover as well, and this tenderness definitely comes across in this movingly translucent instrumental. It somehow makes me feel as if I am up there in the capsule of Sputnik 2, along with Laika, back in those far-off days of the late-1950s. It's a moving interlude.

'Charmed Life' (Hannon)

This love song to Neil Hannon's recently born daughter, Willow, makes for a touching ending to the *Absent Friends* album. Mostly in 4/4 time, with occasional bars of 2/4, the piano playing evinces a strong ragtime feel with a swaying, semiquaver lilt to it. Fairly chord-intensive, it's a gorgeous song built on two basic sections: the first is a verse that ends with a lovely descending vocal melisma on the song title, acting as a kind of chorus. It is lovingly crooned by Hannon and contains some delicious chord shifts beneath his velvety vocal, starting from an F and moving via a Bb13 (#11), an Fm6 to G and then, finally, landing back in the home key of C.

The second section of the song moves to Db, as Hannon reflects on the ups and downs of his life so far and comes to the conclusion that he has ended up in a better place, reiterated in the verses, where he celebrates his 'Charmed Life'. The first repeat of the Db section sees him reminiscing over various failed romances and he quotes the line, 'Breaking up is so very hard to do', from The Walker Brothers' 1965 hit single 'Make It Easy On Yourself', proving that the Scott Walker influence is never far away, especially where Mr Hannon is concerned! But his faith in finding 'the one' finally paid off when he met his wife Orla – 'And not long after that, along came you', he then exclaims to his daughter Willow.

Towards the end, the orchestra take up the verse melody with a glorious sweep, underlining what a lovely tune it is. A chromatic rise by the orchestra ushers in another repeat of the Db section, but this time, with huge chromatic orchestral runs up and down, simulating waves, as Hannon equates life to 'being afloat on a raging sea, in a little row-boat'. However, he celebrates the fact that he hasn't been washed overboard and the waves eventually deposit him on a friendly shore – hence the song title, reflecting on his life as a 'Charmed Life'. The track fades out with Hannon singing the song title, while a somewhat dissonant-sounding banjo plunks out a variation on the ragtime piano riff that opened the song. The net effect of this closing track is, as you might expect – charming!

Additional Tracks

'Idaho' (Hannon)

While on a solo tour of America supporting Ben Folds in 2002, Hannon wrote this song while visiting the state capital of Idaho, the town of Boise (pronounced *boy-see*), on 18 March. A brief return to the UK followed for a recording session at Konk Studios in London during May, where, along with other tracks, 'Idaho' was recorded. Two years later, the song finally appeared on the single 'Come Home Billy Bird'. 'Idaho' is a lovely little ballad in which Hannon gives vent to his homesickness while holed up in a snowy Boise, having been touring the North American continent for several months at that point. Following the UK jaunt for the Konk session, several more months of Stateside touring still lay ahead of him.

The lyrics are personal and from the heart, as Hannon admits he would rather be 'sitting on my sofa with a cup of tea' and 'watching Premiership football, the proper kind'. He plays piano accompaniment and some graceful strings bring out the emotion in the song. As well as his home comforts, he is obviously missing his wife Orla, concluding that, without her, 'this whole world is Boise, Idaho'. The sighing lilt of F to Fm on the word 'Boise', before falling back to C for the verse, gives this tender song an added pathos.

'Mr. Right' (Hannon)

This track was recorded during early sessions for the *Absent Friends* album in October 2002 at Intimate Studios, London. It was eventually released as part of the 'Absent Friends' CD single on 14 June 2004. It sports an intro/bridge section, featuring a horn arrangement that sounds straight out of late-1960s pop, with a strong Burt Bacharach flavour. 'Mr. Right' is a sturdy pop song that positively stomps along via Hannon's propulsive piano and urgent vocals. It's a song about a lack of commitment to a relationship, voiced by someone who is more out for a good time than settling down to family life. The chorus is a catchy one and is clarified by the statement that, despite being more than willing to show said girl a good time, he chants: 'I'm sorry sister/I'm not your Mr. Right'. Although not a major DC track, it's a worthwhile pop tune that will sneak into your brain to mentally replay itself after a couple of listens.

Victory For The Comic Muse (2006)

Personnel:
Neil Hannon: vocals, keyboards, acoustic guitar, electric guitar, banjo, arrangements
Simon Little: bass, double bass
Andrew Skeet: piano, harpsichord, additional arrangements
John Evans: acoustic guitar, electric guitar
Rob Farrer: percussion
Dougie Payne: bass
Tim Weller: drums
Lucy Wilkins, Andrew Haveron, Gillon Cameron, Rick Koster, Alison Dods, Calina De La Mare, Anna Kirkpatrick, Ruth Rogers, Sonia Slany: violin
Reiad Chibah, John Metcalfe: viola
Chris Worsey, Ian Burdge: cello
Charlotte Glasson: baritone saxophone, tenor saxophone
Daniel Newell: trumpet
Mike Kearsey: trombone
Matthew Gunner: French horn
Eliza Marshall: flute
Chris Richards: clarinet
Ilid Jones: oboe, cor anglais
Celine Saout, Camilla Pay: harp
Ian Watson: accordion
Recorded at RAK Studios, London between 4 December 2005 and March 2006
Mixed at Strongroom Studios, Shoreditch, London
Engineers: Richard Woodcraft, Raj Das, Lawrence Aldridge (RAK) and Mark Bishop (Strongroom)
Producer: Neil Hannon
Mastered by Steve Rooke at Abbey Road Studios, London
Record label: Parlophone
Released: 19 June 2006
Highest UK chart position: 43

During 2004, The Divine Comedy toured using several different formats – the first of these was in April when an orchestral tour with The Millennia Strings was followed in May by a stripped-down trio tour, where Neil Hannon was joined by Danny Sheridan on piano and Rory Pierce on cello. June saw a Festival tour by a newly formed line-up, as Hannon hit the road with John Evans on guitar, Ian Watson on accordion, Simon Little on double bass, Andrew Skeet on keyboards, Lucy Wilkins on violin, Rob Farrer on percussion and Tim Weller on drums. This configuration would form the bedrock of personnel that would record the next DC album with Hannon.

On 14 November 2004, Neil Hannon joined a selection of the current crop of pop glitterati, as Bob Geldof and Midge Ure oversaw a new recording of their famous 1984 charity song: 'Do They Know It's Christmas'. This was released on 29 November under the group name Band Aid 20 and reached number one in the UK singles chart in December.

In January 2005, Neil Hannon commenced work on material for a new DC album at home in Dublin. In March, he was back at RAK Studios in London, recording vocals for a Joby Talbot track – 'So Long & Thanks For All The Fish' – one of the songs to be featured on the soundtrack of a film version of Douglas Adams' sci-fi comedy classic *The Hitch-Hiker's Guide To The Galaxy*. Joby Talbot had provided the soundtrack to this film, which premiered on 29 April 2005.

Throughout December, Hannon directed sessions for the new DC album, as yet still untitled, at RAK Studios. The approach this time was to try and record everything as live as possible and to go down the analogue route, using 2-inch reel-to-reel tape and be as 'old school' as could be achieved in the modern age. By 20 December, all the music for the album had been recorded, and in January 2006, Hannon returned to RAK Studios to add his vocals to the recordings, with Guy Massey engineering. After the duo had mixed the album through February, it was completed in March.

The album artwork features a series of stylised stamps with portraits of Hannon – the one on the front cover shows him as a victorious racing driver of times past, with a cheering, hat-waving crowd around him. Other stamp portraits in the CD booklet portray him as a scientist with beakers and test tubes and also as a mountaineer. These all represented him as something of an adventurous explorer, which, in a musical sense, he was and always had been.

Meanwhile, on 6 March, Neil Hannon became the recipient of the James Joyce Award, bestowed by the Literary and Historical Society of University College, Dublin, for standing out 'as an original voice in an industry otherwise full of bland sound-alikes' – quite an honour!He had also kept himself busy penning songs for other artists. These included a song for veteran songstress Jane Birkin, featured on her album *Fictions*, released on 27 March and to which Hannon had contributed the song 'Home'. He also undertook some songwriting sessions with Guy Chambers (famous for his work with Robbie Williams) and two of these songs emerged on the Laura Michelle Kelly album *The Storm Inside*, released on 1 May 2006. The two songs in question were the title track and 'Butterflies'.

When the new DC album was released on 19 June 2006, it was now titled *Victory For The Comic Muse* (yet another Hannon reference to his novelist hero EM Forster). Despite the huge amount of love, skill and hard work put into creating this album, the media reception was muted and sales failed to reflect the brilliance of this latest Hannon masterwork. The best media review came from the French magazine *Les Inrockuptables*, who observed, 'Neil Hannon continues his atemporal, baroque and always refined exploration of pop', while mainstream UK music publications were less charitable. Mat Snow in *Mojo* thought it 'a touch too ITV costume drama' but conceded that it can 'prove highly agreeable in small doses'. Stephen Trousse, in *Uncut,* opined of Hannon: 'He can't recapture the audacious conceits or raptures of *Liberation* and *Promenade*'. Personally, I can't understand music journalists' reluctance at the time to embrace what is clearly one of The Divine Comedy's most subtle and well-crafted musical statements yet. The album spent a couple of weeks on the UK chart and only managed to climb to number 43 in the listings. Neil Hannon must have been extremely disappointed with this chart showing at the time and the singles from the album proved to be the last two forays into the UK singles chart by The Divine Comedy to date. 'Diva Lady' spent two weeks on the chart, topping at number 52 in June, and 'To Die A Virgin' only managed one week at number 67 in August. The latter was issued as a 7" single, a maxi-CD and a download bundle via iTunes – the last of these also contained a Hannon instrumental: 'Pamplemousse'.

'To Die A Virgin' (Hannon)

All the members of the band playing together simultaneously (with no headphones!) caused a few headaches on this session – as revealed on the DVD 'The Divine Comedy's Mysterious World', issued as a bonus disc with the CD release of the album. This approach did eventually lend many of the tracks on the album a satisfyingly cohesive feel and drive, once things clicked into place. With a stomping piano and string-driven beat, the choruses are built on a descending chromatic bass line and decorated with John Evans' slide guitar to emphasise the downward slope of this sequence. The ELO influence, again, comes through strongly on this recording. Some catchy 'Sha-la-la-la-la' backing vocals make the choruses more sing-along-friendly and the live energy is contagious.

The lyrics explore the syndrome of adolescent sexual frustration and the anxiety of getting laid as soon as possible, just in case of inadvertently ending up dying while still a virgin. The track opens with speech samples of actress Jennifer Ehle and actor Toby Stephens, playing a couple discussing virginity. It was sampled from the Channel 4 TV series *The Camomile Lawn* – a drama set at the commencement of the Second World War. The protagonist of the song, though, is a modern-day teenager who is apparently on a promise for his birthday and obviously can't wait for some action, getting hot and bothered over one of his brother's magazines in the meantime. This verse gives a name check to a then-popular brand of tissues, via the line: 'The 'Handy Andies' I've been through!'

The other major features of this arrangement are brazen brass riffs and a freewheeling saxophone from Charlotte Glasson, as she throws in some loose-limbed runs, while the track romps ever-forward. The punctuated ending suddenly comes to an unexpected full stop, just short of four minutes in, completing a rousing start to the album.

'Mother Dear' (Hannon)

A song for all those who love their mother dearly – I still love my mum as much as ever, even though she's been gone for many years now, so I'm automatically well-disposed towards this song. Hannon's affection for his mother shines through brightly in this sprightly tune, powered by some delicious banjo picking from the main man himself. It's an instrument that featured more and more frequently in later-period Divine Comedy recordings and it sounds positively joyous on this track. It's a catchy tune that may have made a better choice for a single than those selected, especially if it had been issued around Mother's Day!

With large doses of Hannon's usual wit and wisdom, the lyrics are simultaneously moving and amusing. This is especially true of the third verse, where he claims that, if he was ever arrested by the CIA, they wouldn't need a polygraph test to obtain the truth; to acquire a confession, they just need to make him look into his mother's eyes, as 'She can see inside'. The notion of the mother figure as a psychological 'safe harbour' for a man is a subject he will return to and expand on with the deeply moving 'When A Man Cries' from the 2010 album *Bang Goes The Knighthood*.

'Diva Lady' (Hannon)

Big, bright piano chords open this track, with beautifully recorded cello lines moving beneath them. These piano chords form the main riff through the verses, enhanced by some tasty conga playing from Rob Farrer, alongside the drums of Tim Weller. The feel on this track sounds similar to a Nile Rodgers production for Chic, especially with the employment of tubular bells, although the bass is less funky than Chic were wont to be. It's insistent, propulsive and very commercial, with a hooky backing vocal chant adding to its chart appeal – it is surprising, therefore, that it wasn't a bigger hit single when it preceded the album in the summer of 2006. The chord progression is simpler than most Hannon fare – while the verses move around an Am-D7-Em sequence, there is a doubled-up middle eight with a two-chord sequence of Dm6 to Am9, the only variation from the verse piano chords, although it is rhythmically identical to the verses.

The identity of the 'Diva Lady' in question remains a mystery, although I'm sure it reflects the demeanour of many an overpaid pop star, displaying the kind of bratty traits mused on in this song.

'A Lady Of A Certain Age' (Hannon)

With John Evans' finger-picked acoustic guitar panned to one side of the stereo mix and Neil Hannon's strummed acoustic guitar chords panned to the other side, this leaves ample space between the two for Hannon's tender vocals on this affecting ballad. The subject is an Englishwoman who was, back in the day, part of high society and is now attempting to age gracefully. The orchestration is again panned out to either side of the sound picture, with a swirling, eddying feel to the orchestral arrangement that works on a hypnotic, repeated pattern of notes in one channel and sweeping strings in the other channel as the vocals unfold the story in the centre. It's a beautiful song and has been compared, lyrically, to Peter Sarstedt's 1969 number one hit single 'Where Do You Go To My Lovely?', although, musically, it's a lot more complex than that song.

The mention of 'Noel's parties by Lake Geneva' in the lyrics is an obvious nod to an ongoing Hannon influence in the shape of Noel Coward. The lyrics explore the life story of the lady in question, moving from the heady days of chasing the sun around the French Riviera, through marriage to a rich partner and the inevitable children. They are packed off to finishing school but end up as something of a disappointment, and eventually, her husband leaves her for 'his mistress in Marseilles'. An underlying sadness permeates this captivating ballad, but also a sense of resignation and a feeling of sad regret at the passing of the lady's halcyon salad days. The full arrangement falls back to just the picked acoustic guitar to close the song – another delightful touch.

'The Light Of Day' (Hannon)

This slow-paced, but gently flowing song opens with two bars of arpeggio harpsichord semiquavers, played by Andrew Skeet, and this instrument forms the main matrix for this touchingly sad, but ultimately hopeful love song. Much of this song's yearning appeal lies in the major seventh and suspended chords it is built on, giving the track an engagingly warm feel that, when combined with Hannon's rich baritone vocals, draws the listener into the story. The verses are sadly reflective, as Hannon sings of perusing old photographs picturing a love affair in happier times 'Before life waded in and tore it all apart'. The chorus, however, is hopeful, with an always-one-more-tomorrow vibe and a conviction that, despite the dark nights of regret, all will eventually become resolved in the bright light of day.

The orchestration is rich and opulent, with the distinctive sound of an oboe rising to the surface on the waves of strings during the middle instrumental passage. It's the harpsichord that lends this track its strong character, though, and there is some fascinating film footage on the bonus DVD that accompanies the CD album. It highlights the difficulty of keeping the harpsichord in tune with the other musicians, as Andrew Skeet attempts to re-tune the numerous strings involved. As is evident from the finished track, though, all tuning problems were happily resolved and the result is one of the most beautiful of Hannon's numerous love ballads.

'Threesome' (Hannon)

This delightfully frisky piano piece is so called as it is performed by three players seated at the same piano: Andrew Skeet at the bass end, Neil Hannon taking the higher lines and John Evans sandwiched between the two of them. Recorded live, this lightly tripping exercise in 6/8 time makes for a refreshingly upbeat instrumental interlude, demonstrating Hannon's easy way with rhythm and melody. In its own way, 'Threesome' is a perfect little pocket masterpiece of form that underlines Hannon's eclectic compositional ability. A live take of this performance is included on the *Mysterious World* DVD that accompanies the CD release of the album.

'Party Fears Two' (Mackenzie, Rankine)
The only cover version on a Divine Comedy album (although some covers were issued on singles and EPs), 'Party Fears Two' was a number nine hit single in the UK charts in February 1982 for The Associates. This post-punk duo comprised of vocalist Billy McKenzie and guitarist Alan Rankine, and they had a string of hit singles and albums in the early 1980s. This being Neil Hannon's teenage era, their influence seeped in, along with other contemporary 1980s pop bands. It's a song with a fascinating structure, both musically and lyrically, starting with the convoluted opening riff, which recurs throughout the song. On the original, this is played on synthesiser, but here, it opens with an enthusiastic string section playing its twisting melody, joined by Rob Farrer making a grand entrance on vibraphone, along with the drums. The riff alone is a clever piece of composing, as its quaver and semiquaver slither over a chord sequence in C major, giving it a sinuous, snaking feel that marks it out as unusual and original. The rhythm adopted for this arrangement is the classic DC galloping snare drum, a rhythm so heavily favoured by Hannon that, in the 'making of' documentary DVD, he jokes that it 'will probably be on my tombstone'. It's the perfect rhythm for this song and gives it considerable forward momentum. The brass section provide a distinct 'oom-pah' feel to the bass end of this arrangement, giving a satisfying balance to this driving track.

The lyrics don't readily make much sense, but they are full of riveting imagery and possess an almost poetic flow to them. Lines like, 'The alcohol loves you, while turning you blue' and 'Even a slight remark, makes no sense it turns to shark', may not make much logical sense in themselves, but once combined with the music, feel absolutely right. Hannon's vocal performance brings out the best in this song and it sounds like he's having a ball singing it. To my ears, there is something of a Spanish feel about the music and this is accentuated by some ascending piano flourishes, the employment of castanets and an E to FMaj7 chord shift that lends a distinct Iberian feel to the bridge section – a device often used in flamenco music.

'Arthur C. Clarke's Mysterious World' (Hannon)
To my ears, this is the catchiest track on the album and would have made an excellent choice for a single. The tune is powered along by Neil Hannon and John Evans strumming acoustic guitars with capos on the neck; as these two instruments mesh, the sound is akin to that of a balalaika. The drum rhythm

has a Latin touch about it, in a tempo and rhythm similar to the classic Doc Pomus/Mort Shuman song 'Save The Last Dance For Me', a worldwide hit for The Drifters in 1960. Some trumpet riffs and fanfares enhance the Latin flavour of the music as the arrangement builds, and there are further traces of ELO in the string department. Sticking to mainly major chords in the verses, with a contrasting middle section moving to a minor chord, this tune haunts the subconscious after a few listens.

Lyrically, the song refers to the 13-part 1980s TV series of the same name, which was introduced by noted science fiction author Arthur C. Clarke, who was filmed at his home in Sri Lanka welcoming the viewer to his 'Mysterious World'. The series was narrated by contemporary TV newsreader Gordon Honeycomb. These programmes looked at unexplained phenomena from around the world. Incidentally, back in 1968, when I was a 13-year-old space fanatic, my school friend Steve Squirrell and I were both members of the British Astronomical Association (a group for amateur astronomers). During one of the BAA meetings at Burlington House, Piccadilly, we both had the honour of meeting and conversing with Arthur C. Clarke (along with Patrick Moore) in the BAA library, following a speech the great man had given on the subject of 'Clarke orbits' for geostationary Earth satellites. However, in this song, it's not geostationary satellites that are on Hannon's mind as needing an explanation, but rather, the enigmatic behaviour of his female companion, who leaves him in a state of bewilderment – hence his plea to include her in any potential new series of the classic TV show about unexplained phenomena. It makes for an amusing lyric, as she proceeds to bamboozle him with subjects, such as the finite-but-unbounded nature of the expanding universe and, as he claims, 'It's like she's speaking in Swahili' and, in a later verse, pondering that his girl is 'as deep as the Baltic Sea'.

As the song switches to a minor chord for a superbly constructed 18-bar middle section, he balances his previous claims by averring his undying love for her, despite her 'mass of contradictions' and 'strange convictions'. In the end, he concludes that 'love doesn't make distinctions'. The result is a refreshingly oblique love song that amuses and delights.

'The Plough' (Hannon)

Definitely the epic of the album, 'The Plough' has a very classical arrangement, with the linking instrumental passages driven by a brazen melody played by the string section of the orchestra, and built on minor sevenths and ninths. It is set against bouncing timpani beats, emphasising the track's bold 6/8 rhythm. These passages have the sort of dramatic, widescreen demeanour that harks back to some of the huge orchestral arrangements Hannon previously employed on *Fin De Siecle*. One of the other hallmarks of this track is its fine attention to dynamics – one moment loud and audacious, the next quiet and contemplative. This led to one or two issues when attempting to stick to the original game plan of recording live with no headphones; in terms of timing and dynamics, the orchestra depended very much on Andrew Skeet's prodigious conducting skills.

Initially, the vocal parts of this track trace their intensifying melodic line over the same minor chords as the opening instrumental passage. However, they build towards a climactic second part that reaches its peak on a tense flattened fifth chord, amplifying the drama of the song and cueing in a dynamic dip that hushes the arrangement down for the punch line of each verse – the couplet, 'I'll plough my own furrow/I'll go my own way'.

The song itself is a kind of three-part morality tale, and a paean to independent thinking and the rejection of different kinds of dogma. It proceeds via three, two-part verses of interlinking stories. The first tells of the protagonist's employment with a firm of accountants. He eventually discovers one of the employees 'massaging the figures for personal gain' and forswears the whole 'house of shame', asserting the conviction of ploughing his own furrow from now on. Low in the mix, there are subtle typewriter sound effects in this verse, conjuring the requisite office ambience.

The second verse involves the sermons of a certain Reverend McBride down at the mission house, where the fire-and-brimstone preacher proceeds to damn to eternal torment all of those who don't know of or follow his particular faith. This is, of course, rejected by our protagonist as a nonsensical notion with the line, 'The stars that we follow can lead us astray', and he, again, avers his determination to 'plough his own furrow' and reject this religious dogma.

After a further instrumental interlude of the string-led passage, a third verse finds our protagonist wandering up in the hills, in what sounds like some South American 'banana republic'. He joins up with a band of guerrillas and is tasked with killing the Chief of Police, but on breaking into the abode of said official, he suddenly sees the potential victim's young infant and desists, realising that 'You murder tomorrow by killing today'. At this point, the dramatic arrangement falls back from a blaring flattened fifth chord for the final, quieter affirmation of ploughing his own furrow – rejecting the way of violence, just as he previously repudiated religious dogma and the corrupting influence that money can have over people. The track plays out gently with the plaintive melody performed by Eliza Marshall on her flute, concluding a rivetingly ambitious arrangement full of power and melodrama.

'Count Grassi's Passage Over Piedmont' (Hannon)

The second of a trio of tracks closing the album that explore different aspects of 6/8 time, this is possibly the most intricately constructed track of all. The song opens by employing the minimalist principle of a short, slowly evolving melodic phrase – initially stated on piano, but throughout the song, taken up and developed by a variety of orchestral instruments, with many subtle modulations. As well as piano and drums, this ingenious arrangement is scored for two clarinets, two violins, cello, French horn, trombone, tuba, glockenspiel, accordion and even that rarely heard wind instrument: the ocarina (in pop, most famously known for taking the solo spot on The Troggs' 1966 hit 'Wild Thing').

The inspired combination of a 6/8 time signature, crisply rolling snare drum and a brilliant orchestral arrangement gives the illusion that the track is moving in a vertical direction, rather than a horizontal one – ideal for a song about a hot-air balloon voyage. The fine musical detail is akin to the 'Faberge egg' that the Count's balloon is likened to in the lyrics. That initial piano phrase assumes heroic proportions once taken up and expanded on by the orchestra. On some of the brass figures especially, the music echoes the style of composer Gustav Holst (especially 'Jupiter' from *The Planets' Suite*).

The poetic lyrics draw the listener into the tale of Count Grassi's balloon trip over Northern Italy and beyond, with geographical mentions of the Alps, the River Po, Padua, the Adriatic Sea and the far-flung destinations of Corsica and Catalonia. However, the Count seems intent on only one thing – more height. To increase the balloon's elevation, it seems as if anything goes; supplies of provisions and wine are dumped overboard to lighten the balloon's load in the quest to ascend ever higher. In his obsession, the Count ponders on a perfect demise: that of plunging from a great height on a warm July afternoon (giving a distinct impression that he may be mentally unstable). However, today's quest is more obviously a stratospheric one, as eventually, a flock of high-flying swallows (brilliantly evoked by a fluttering woodwind figure) metaphorically warn him back with the line, 'Go back from whence you came'. Furthermore, they accuse the Count (and by implication, the human race) of bad stewardship of the planet via the warning, 'You've corrupted and befouled the ground you walk upon', obviously fearing the same fate for their own abode: the skies. This encounter seems to shame Count Grassi, who utters, 'Please friends, forgive this intrusion'. Here, Hannon is returning to a green agenda, initially expressed as far back as the very first DC album in 1990 (in the songs 'Tailspin' and 'Logic v Emotion'). The way Hannon performs this track vocally is quite extraordinary, utilising both singing and recitation, as spoken lines are reflected by overlapping sung lines.

There are many resonant poetic phrases contained within the engrossing lyrics that bring to life the saga of Count Grassi's relentless quest for more altitude. My personal favourite is: 'O Newton, release this apple from its Earthly shackles'. This is a clear reference to the apocryphal story involving the 17th-century mathematician and astronomer Sir Isaac Newton, who is said to have deduced his gravitational theory after watching an apple fall from a tree.

This is a song that is as much a voyage of discovery as Count Grassi's revelatory balloon trip, as the rich subtleties of this intricately constructed gem of a track unveil themselves with subsequent listens.

'Snowball In Negative' (Hannon)

The last of the trio of studies in 6/8 time that closes the album, this is yet another treasure trove of subtlety. It opens with a faint, modulating, buzzing hum that sounds as if it may have been electronically generated. A phrase played on the celesta takes over from this, along with pizzicato violin plucking, over which Neil Hannon's treated vocal is laid. His layered vocal sound is close to the style employed by ex-Genesis guitarist Steve Hackett on his excellent album *Wild Orchids*, recorded the same year as *Victory For The Comic Muse*. The song moves along in an understated way, although the orchestral arrangement is, again, extremely intricate. As well as celesta and two violins, it also takes in accordion, clarinet, French horn, cello, viola, oboe, piano, trombone, percussion and harpsichord. The vocal melody is lilting and rather lovely and the verses are split with a series of piano triplet cascades, which move to 4/4 time via a bar of 3/8. These lightly tripping, descending lines are played at the higher end of the keyboard. There is much fine orchestral detail underpinning the verses and it's one of those tracks that demands repeated listens to absorb its many facets – but it is well worth the effort.

Lyrically, Neil Hannon is pondering on entropy and slow decay – in the first verse, watching the ash from his '600th last cigarette' roll away, ever-diminishing and comparing this to a 'Snowball In Negative' – fading away rather than accumulating. The second verse brings further reflections on the entropic process, as applied to human life: 'Giving and giving and slowly diminishing' until all that's left of us is 'ash in the breeze'. A sombre subject, to be sure, but very much a part of our existence and that of everything else we know of. On this bleak note, the track returns to the piano cascades, with the orchestra building over the top until the piano comes to a rest. Several bars later, the album ends with a resounding high E and low B played simultaneously on the piano – in effect, Hannon's 'A Day In The Life' moment (although, nowhere near as heavy on the pedal, or long in duration, as that on The Beatles' masterpiece).

Additional Material

'Don't Blame The Young' (Hannon)

Musically, this medium-tempo song in 12/8 works as a parody of the 1950s blues-based, piano-led ballad style. The opening strongly recalls that of The Bonzo Dog Doo-Dah Band's 1968 comic masterpiece 'The Canyons Of Your Mind' (the B-side to their chart hit 'I'm The Urban Spaceman'). Hannon's piano is augmented by honking saxophones as he beseeches one and all not to blame the youth of the world for its problems. It's a highly amusing lyric with some deliciously funny moments. I particularly like the couplet: 'They're wedded to their mobiles: you can't turn the damn thing on'. There is a brass-enhanced chorus where he pleads with teachers and parents not to give the young such a hard time, because, soon enough, their youth will be behind them. There is a piano solo, hammered out and sticking rigidly to the sequence, with a few glissandos thrown in. The ending has a classic turnaround, as Hannon, again, urges us not to blame the young, adding the aside, 'you can pity them – but don't blame the young'. The song was originally released on the 'Diva Lady' CD single on 12 June 2006.

'Births, Deaths And Marriages' (Hannon)
This song was released on the 'Diva Lady' CD2 single, along with the pleasant, if unessential, Hannon instrumental 'Premonition Of Love'. Opening with a swaying string prelude that is quite lovely, Hannon soon takes over with jaunty, rhythmic piano chords that instantly recall Paul McCartney's piano part in the middle section of The Beatles' 'A Day In The Life'. This marvellously upbeat song also has a banjo plunking away somewhere in the mix. As the song develops, it starts to take on a New Orleans jazz-band feel, courtesy of a swinging brass section cutting loose. There is a brief pregnant pause mid-song before a cute vibraphone run swings it back into the stomping rhythm once more, underpinned by a four-beats-to-the-bar bass drum.

Hannon's lyrics are mostly humorous reflections on life. In the first verse, he comments on his own busy schedule, with 'Commitments squeezed like tinned sardines', but all is well in Hannon-land, as 'Where there's life, there's generally a bar', to which he yells, 'Line 'em up'. The chorus invokes the births, deaths and marriages of the title, along with 'Cabbages and kings', as well as 'Slugs and snails and spam emails'. In the second of the upbeat, catchy choruses, he comes up with the droll couplet: 'I'm not from Venus or from Mars, I'm from Enniskillen!'

There are many other amusing lyrics to savour as this jaunty confection stomps its jolly way along. The ending brings a further smile to this listener's face, as, over a held note from the brass – and amid some luscious flute and clarinet trills – Hannon announces to one and all, Dave Allen-style: 'Goodnight, and may your God go with you'. Wonderful!

'Long Slow Suicide' (Hannon)
A slow-paced, late-1960s ballad feel returns once more as some deep piano notes open proceedings, supported by acoustic string bass and staccato guitar chords. The lyric ponders on those things we enjoy that inevitably degrade our health and the chances of a longer existence. Hannon sings of enjoying a smoke, watching his favourite football team, eating fried food and drinking too much, before coming to the conclusion that all these pursuits 'take a day off my life', equating this in the chorus to 'a long, slow, suicide'. The descending sequence of this chorus suits the lyrics perfectly in this neat, thoughtful, but slightly disconsolate song. It first appeared on the B-side of the 7" single 'To Die A Virgin', released on 14 August 2006.

'Absolute Power' (Hannon)
Pizzicato violins accompany Neil Hannon's vocals on the opening verse of this song of reflection on the perils and pitfalls of fame. As the song

progresses, a pair of staccato guitar strokes accentuate the offbeat on the second half of each bar, recalling The Walker Brothers yet again. Some understated orchestration enhances this mid-paced production, and when the choruses arrive, there is a tangible soul feel to the music.

Lyrically, the song is based on the maxim, 'Absolute power corrupts absolutely', as Hannon's ruminations on fame finally arrive at the conclusion: 'Fame doesn't care if you live or die'. This track appeared on the maxi-CD format of 'To Die A Virgin'.

'Miss Sharapova' (Hannon)

Another instrumental experiment, this fascinating little gem, opens with a repeating electric piano cascade, joined by a prodding synthesised bass. There's some nice reverb-tinged percussion with repeat echoes and a rising string pad supporting this as the track moves forward. The most incisive section is a dose of sustained Robert Fripp-like guitar playing the melody, after which the track falls back to the cascading electric piano sound that opened it. It was first made available on the digital download bundle, along with 'Lady Of A Certain Age' and a live version of 'Sticks & Stones', on 6 November 2006.

The Duckworth Lewis Method (2009)

Personnel:
Neil Hannon: vocals, piano, vocoder, Mellotron, Korg, organ, electric guitar, acoustic guitar, harpsichord, woodwind, strings, electric 12-string guitar, glockenspiel, face percussion, banjo, tubular bells, car, cello, zither, tambourine
Thomas Walsh: vocals, electric guitar, Mellotron, acoustic guitar, percussion, 'cricket bat' bass drum, kazoo, yawn, third hand (!), counting, drums
Keith Farrell: bass, electric guitar, upright bass, greetings, drums, backing vocals, whistle, micro-counting
Johnny Boyle: drums
Tosh Flood: electric guitar, backing vocals
Cathy Davey: vocals ('The Sweet Spot' and 'Test Match Special')
Matt Berry: monologue ('Out On The Boundary')
Matt Lunson: vocals, backing vocals
Tim Weller: drums ('Test Match Special')
The Twelfth Men: claps
Neil Hannon, Phil Jupitus, Matt Berry, Alexander Armstrong, Jonathan Brigden, Ciaran Little, Chris Worsey, Rob Farrer, Andrew Skeet and Cecelia Lewis: baboon chorus ('Jiggery Pokery')
Millenia Strings ('The Nightwatchman'): Everton Nelson (leader), Patrick Kiernan, Lucy Wilkins, Perry Montague-Mason, Warren Zielinski: first violins
Richard George, Natalia Bonner, Alison Dods, Gillon Cameron: second violins
Bruce White, Reiad Chibah, Morgan Goff: viola
Chris Worsey, Ian Burdge, Frank Schaeffer: cello
Mary Scully: double bass
Andrew Skeet: Millennia Strings conductor
Recorded at The Bunker, Neil's Place and Exchequer Studios, Dublin and RAK Studios, London (baboon chorus on 'Jiggery Pokery')
Mixed at The Bunker by Keith Farrell, assisted by Neil Hannon and Thomas Walsh
Date: February 2008 – April 2009
Engineer: Keith Farrell
Additional Engineering: Guy Massey, assisted by Richard Woodcraft
Produced and arranged by Neil Hannon and Thomas Walsh
Mastered by Geoff Pesche at Abbey Road Studios, London
Record label: Divine Comedy Records
Released: 5 July 2009
Highest UK chart position: 40

Following Neil Hannon's first meeting with Thomas Walsh in October 2003, the pair kept in touch, and by 2006, were recording together for the Pugwash & Friends' Christmas song 'Tinsel And Marzipan', released on 8 December 2006 in the hope of achieving a Yuletide hit. By May 2007, they were back in the studio, along with ex-XTC guitarist Dave Gregory (who was later to grace progressive rock band Big Big Train) and XTC main man Andy Partridge,

who co-wrote two songs with Walsh: 'My Genius' and 'At The Sea'. He also contributed Swanee whistle, kazoo, Mellotron and acoustic guitar to the latter track. Neil Hannon played on ten of the 11 tracks that made up the new Pugwash album *Eleven Modern Antiquities*, providing vocals, zither harp, glockenspiel, vocoder, piano, organ and synthesiser as part of the ensemble.

By 2007, Hannon's marriage to Orla had sadly run its course as the couple drifted further apart romantically, although they remained close friends. It was at a reception for the new Pugwash album that he first met his new love interest: musician and singer Cathy Davey. She would make musical contributions to many of Hannon's future releases.

In February 2008, Hannon and Walsh began recording demos at Hannon's place for their new joint project – The Duckworth Lewis Method. This was planned to be a concept album of sorts, as all the songs would pertain to the game of cricket. Their snappy moniker was adopted from the cricketing term of the same name, devised by statisticians Frank Duckworth and Tony Lewis, and introduced into the game in 1997. It was formally adopted by the ICC in 1999 and represented a mathematical formulation designed to calculate the number of runs needed to win for the team batting second in a one-day cricket match, in the event of interruption from inclement weather.

Throughout the rest of 2008, the pair worked on the album, mainly at The Bunker in Dublin and the official announcement of their new project together took place in January 2009, when several of the tracks were released to the press and on the internet. Additional recording took place at RAK Studios, London, on 4 March for the track 'Jiggery Pokery', and from 2 April to 3 April, the album was mastered at Abbey Road Studios, London.

Over the next few months, the duo did the rounds of radio stations and press junkets, playing a short selection of songs from their debut album. In late June, they were joined by DC regulars, Simon Little on bass and Tim Weller on drums, as rehearsals commenced and tour dates were booked. DLM's live debut was, rather fittingly, in the Long Room at Lord's Cricket Ground, prior to the Surrey v Middlesex game! More dates followed, including a gig at The Oval on 7 July, where the set was bolstered by Hannon's greatest hit – 'National Express', the Pugwash song 'It's Nice To Be Nice' and Booker T & The MGs' 'Soul Limbo' (the original *BBC Test Match Cricket* theme tune), as well as the complete Duckworth Lewis Method debut album.

The amusing cover artwork displays a graphic of the duo in a flying car with cricket bats extending from either side, as it hovers over a test match in progress below. Their debut proved to be a delicious serving of timeless pop music and was, more than likely, the first cricket-pop album, a leader in a field of one! Even those with no interest in cricket would surely be hooked by the intoxicating brew of catchy tunes, uproarious humour and musical dexterity on display throughout these recordings. The album was deservedly nominated for an Ivor Novello Award in 2010, in the 'Best Album of the Year' category. It was narrowly pipped-at-the-post by Paolo Nutini's *Sunny Side Up*, although Mr Nutini eventually conceded that he thought *The Duckworth Lewis Method* would win, as 'their album was a bit of genius'.

Following the album's release on 5 July 2009, it spent a month on the UK album charts, peaking at number 40. It also drew appreciative comments from ELO's Jeff Lynne (who was a Pugwash fan, as well as an obvious influence on both Hannon and Walsh). The ELO maestro stated to Walsh: 'I really like the cricket album', seemingly becoming part of a mutual admiration society with the DLM duo.

'The Coin Toss' (Hannon, Walsh)

That traditional start of a cricket match, 'The Coin Toss' opens with the mood-enhancing sounds of murmuring voices and bird calls, before Hannon's piano and Mellotron enter with a simple, plaintive riff in triple time. A hard-to-decipher vocoder announces that 'Duckworth and Lewis are here'. Suddenly, we swap to common time and crotchets on piano, as the previously declared duo introduce themselves, starting with a cheery 'Hello!' from Duckworth (Walsh) and a 'Good morning!' from Lewis (Hannon). With a short 1:08 duration arrangement, strong on humour, our intrepid twosome toss a coin to decide which of them will go in for a bat, including the amusing couplet: 'May the best man win' (Duckworth) – 'And may the best Duckworth lose!' (Lewis). Johnny Boyle's drums clatter in halfway through this cheery little tune, and there are some clarinet-like doodles reminiscent of The Beatles' 'When I'm Sixty-Four'. These are probably performed on a Mellotron, as this instrument is played by both Hannon and Walsh on this track. If you're wondering who won the coin toss – it was Lewis!

'The Age Of Revolution' (Hannon, Walsh)

The first download single released from the album, this song charts the rise of cricket in Pakistan in the 20th century, following years of repression that 'started a noise from the street'. The game went from strength to strength after Pakistan gained its independence in 1947. The song celebrates kids in the valleys, using 'bats held together with string'. This particular 'age of revolution' would eventually lead to the world-conquering Pakistani national team becoming leading players on the global stage.

The element that gives this song its extreme catchiness is a repeated 1920s jazz band sample that forms a matrix for the chorus. The track opens and closes with an acapella chant of the song title. There is a strong reggae-rock feel on display, with an electric guitar rhythm on the offbeat. Both Hannon and bassist Keith Farrell play guitars, the latter throwing in a few lead lines as well as providing bass, while both Hannon and Walsh double on vocals. The result is a highly infectious concoction, with a celebratory joy that transfers to the listener, and this upbeat vibe is a hallmark of this largely jovial album.

'Gentlemen And Players' (Hannon, Walsh)
With its gently swaying rhythm and tuneful melody, this paean to Lord's Cricket Ground proves to be an amusing sweep through salient points of the ground's history. The first verse takes us back to 1825, when owner Thomas Lord sold off the cricket ground to Bank of England governor William Ward MP, himself a keen cricketer. The chorus is memorable and celebrates the gentlemen and players who dominated the game in the 19th century, playing on a 'Sunday afternoon' in 'April, May and June'. Hannon handles the lead vocals, while Walsh contributes some lovely backing vocals.

The second verse invokes the eccentric English cricketer Fuller Pilch with his pipe and top hat, who first appeared at Lord's in July 1820, playing for his home county of Norfolk. Hannon paints a vivid portrait of Pilch, who 'comes a cropper' as he 'knocks the bails off with his topper' – it's all highly amusing stuff and sounds terribly English (despite the duo being from Ireland)!

This sumptuous tune has a rhythmic sway similar to The Mamas and The Papas' 1965 hit single 'California Dreamin'' – although melodically different. Hannon is credited with guitar, harpsichord, woodwind and strings, as well as vocals. To my ears, the woodwind and string parts sound as if they are played on a Mellotron. Walsh strums his acoustic guitar and adds some percussion in addition to his backing vocals, while the usual Farrell/Boyle rhythm section is bolstered by some extra guitar from Tosh Flood. The twanging guitar solo on the coda is particularly atmospheric and displays a touch of Vic Flick-style plucking, sonically similar to the *James Bond Theme* guitar sound.

'The Sweet Spot' (Hannon, Walsh)
Basically a 12-bar shuffle, this track kicks along beautifully and has another infectious melody built over its bluesy structure. The Farrell/Boyle rhythm section packs a mighty wallop and both the bass and drums on this album are particularly noteworthy. There are some great unison guitar/bass riffs linking verses together, giving the track its dynamic forward drive. Hannon's employment of the Korg synthesiser is hugely effective here, too, with Theremin-like notes after the first 'Find the sweet spot' chorus, with a panned, phased whooshing after the second chorus, being especially imaginative and giving an added dimension to this rocking song. He throws in some dandy rock 'n' roll piano playing to boot. Hannon and Walsh sing the vocals together and there is a vocal contribution from Hannon's new romantic partner, Cathy Davey.

In cricketing terms, the sweet spot is situated near the end of the cricket bat, where it is at its thickest. In this song, the term appears to have a dual meaning, as the lyric can also be read as a kind of racy love song about hitting the sweet spot during lovemaking! It's another gloriously catchy tune that is hard to resist singing along to.

'Jiggery Pokery' (Hannon, Walsh)

This rib-tickling ode, influenced by English music hall, is performed on just piano, acoustic guitar, upright bass and percussion, and owes a debt to the style of 1960s satirical duo Flanders & Swann. With Hannon's piano guiding its stop/start arrangement, there are many tempo fluctuations for comical effect, which work brilliantly, and the lyric is genuinely funny.

It tells of the moment in the first test of the Ashes at Old Trafford, Manchester, in June 1993, when Australian spin-bowler Shane Warne turned the game of cricket on its head by bowling his so-called 'ball of the century' against Mike Gatting. The song is sung from the perspective of the bewildered England batsman. The match initially seemed to be going well for England, until 'Merv Hughes and his handlebar moustache dismissed poor 'Athers'' (referring to England batsman Mike Atherton). From then on, it was downhill all the way for the home side, as Shane Warne's performance that day changed the course of the match and led to a wider revival of spin-bowling in cricket, over the then-dominant pace-bowling. On the day, Mike Gatting appeared to be momentarily in shock, until the umpire, Dickie Bird, 'slowly raised his finger', indicating that Gatting had been out-bowled by the young Aussie leg-spinner.

The chorus is priceless and expresses Gatting's shock at being bowled out by Warne, via the latter's 'Robbery, muggery, Aussie skullduggery' that put him 'Out for a buggering duck' and made him seem 'Like a blithering old buffoon'. The second chorus amends this last comment to, 'Like an accident-prone baboon' – this cues in the 'baboon chorus', where Hannon is joined by some friends, namely Phil Jupitus, Matt Berry, Alexander Armstrong, Chris Worsey, Rob Farrer, Jonathan Brigden, Ciairan Little, Andrew Skeet and Cecelia Lewis. This jolly choir, plus Hannon, all chant the word 'baboon' over and over on the beat and are credited as 'The Congressional 11' (even though there are 10 of them!). It's a track that is a heap of fun to listen to, and it eventually found its way into The Divine Comedy live set, when Hannon performed his solo tour under the group name in 2010. A live DC version can be heard on the album *Live At Somerset House*, which was released following the 2010 tour.

'Mason On The Boundary' (Hannon, Walsh)

With an intro betraying the influence of The Drifters 1963 worldwide hit single 'On Broadway', this gently undulating tune is sung by Hannon and Walsh over strummed acoustic guitars and electric 12-string – a deliciously mellow creation. Walsh adds Mellotron, while Hannon utilizes his Korg synthesiser; a vocoder is also employed to process the smooth backing vocals. There is some atmospheric lead guitar picking by Tosh Flood to complete the musical picture.

Lyrically, the song is most likely a tribute to legendary cricketer John Richard Mason (also known as Jack Mason), who played for Kent County

Cricket Club between 1893 and 1914. The song appears to be set sometime later, as it paints a portrait of an ageing Mason enjoying a match on a sunny day while 'out on the boundary'. Matt Berry's monologue finds him dozing as he dreams of his old contemporaries: cricketing legends Denis Compton and Don Bradman. He has obviously been imbibing, as there is an expressive depiction of his 'double-malted subconscious' and he wakes as 'the scent of tweed and gingham fill his colonial senses' – all very poetic. There aren't many pop songs that use phrases like 'hopelessly panglossian' – this appears in the final verse, in reference to Mason's overly optimistic outlook, as he gradually fades into the twilight: forever 'out on the boundary'.

'Rain Stops Play' (Hannon, Walsh)
Following Mason's final musing of 'Hmmm – it looks like rain' during Matt Berry's monologue on the previous track, the cumulonimbus clouds slowly gather as 'Rain Stops Play'. Hence this short 1:13 instrumental interlude, on which Hannon and Walsh both play Mellotron, with some nice woodwind sounds in the mix, while Hannon's tinkling glockenspiel imitates a cascading rain shower. The arrangement moves from a fast, shuffling beat to a more static-sounding middle passage before returning briefly to its speedy shuffle, then down-turning into an unexpected final suspension. On DLM's 2013 tour, certain members of the band would mill about on the stage whirling umbrellas on this number.

'Meeting Mr. Miandad' (Hannon, Walsh)
The second single release from the album, this simple but perfect pop song deserved to be a smash hit, although sadly, it failed to chart. In any vote for the happiest-sounding, feel-good record of all time, this compelling confection should be right up there with ELO's 'Mr. Blue Sky' (which *was* voted the happiest song of all time in a poll!). Once heard a few times, it's one of those pop tunes that is virtually impossible not to end up whistling – a real earworm. Opening with eight crashing, descending piano chords that lead into its bouncy reggae-pop groove, it jogs along with a jaunty feel and features several clever modulations at various points, that lift the key of the song higher and higher, as it moves through its 3:12 duration. Hannon sings the verses and is joined by Walsh on the choruses, as they reprise their roles as Duckworth (Walsh) and Lewis (Hannon).

The song starts with the duo waking early one morning and deciding to set off on a cricketing pilgrimage to Pakistan, in an attempt to meet Pakistani cricket coach, commentator and former cricketer Javed Miandad – often hailed as one of the greatest batsmen in the history of the game. He played for the national team between 1975 and 1996. In this verse, Lewis awakes from a dream in which Mr. Miandad has 'called' him, so he phones a yawning Duckworth, with the declaration: 'Pack up your bags, we're going to Pakistan'. This leads into the first of the song's irresistible choruses, which become more intoxicating as the song progresses, complete with downward swooping backing vocals that underline the strong ELO influence on this tune.

In the second verse, Lewis describes the journey as they head eastwards in their VW Camper Van. This verse has some deliciously humorous couplets on display, my particular favourites being: 'Everywhere we go, people know us' (with a cheery 'Hello!' in a Brummie-sounding accent in the background, that sounds a dead-ringer for Jeff Lynne's voice!) and 'When we break down, people tow us', with Hannon adding the 'car' sound effect noted in the earlier credits. These lovely little touches bring to mind the carefully crafted pop singles of the late 1960s, that similarly employed sound effects to enhance the atmosphere and storyline of songs such as the Small Faces' 'Lazy Sunday' and The Beatles' 'Penny Lane', amongst many others.

After a return of the eight descending piano chords that opened the song, the key modulates up for a third verse, with massed handclaps and a triumphant downbeat – this verse charts the duo's arrival in Pakistan and their meeting with the cricketing legend. After getting there and shaking his hand, their hero says: 'Wait there while I get my guitar, I'm a rock 'n' roll star like you, Woo-hoo-hoo!' This is followed by another of those ecstatic choruses that wind down to Lewis singing the line: 'It's our historical, phantasmagorical, destiny'.

Just when you think the song is over, there is a jolly coda – with Hannon on banjo – played jug band-style. It's a track that's a bundle of fun, as well as being a terrific pop song in the classic tradition.

'The Nightwatchman' (Hannon, Walsh)

The poignant moment of the album is up next, in the shape of this Hannon-sung ballad. He accompanies himself on piano and the arrangement is given added gravitas by an appearance of The Millennia Strings, conducted by Andrew Skeet, consisting of nine violins, three violas and three cellos, along with Mary Scully on double bass. The string arrangement is reminiscent of ELO crossed with a 1970s Philly-soul feel, which suits the tune admirably.

The song takes its name from *The Wisden Cricket Quarterly* publication *The Nightwatchman*, but the lyrics come over more like a sad love song of great longing, in which the protagonist lies awake 'Fighting the ghosts and the demons inside my head'. The chorus promises his longed-for lover, 'All that I have is yours', and the unremitting minor key emphasises the intense yearning on display here. Tosh Flood weighs in with some delicate wah-wah guitar, along with Hannon's piano and the keening strings, in a heavily atmospheric performance. It's a track that provides a necessary contrast to the jollier, upbeat pop that dominates this DLM debut album. There is a lovely, bluesy piano solo from Hannon towards the end, leading into a string-led coda that sports a classical grace, with strong minor chords, making for a heartrending finale to this touching ode.

'Flatten The Hay' (Hannon, Walsh)
Thomas Walsh takes the lead vocal for this reflective, triple-time pastoral idyll, which conjures up long-ago Irish summers spent with his brother. When it came to sporting pastimes, the cricket-mad brothers inevitably plumped for the 'gentleman's game' over football or golf. The easy swing of the verses firms up for the repeated middle eight and the whole thing recalls the writing style of Andy Partridge of XTC, one of Walsh's personal heroes. It's a fascinating and thoroughly engaging track and benefits greatly from Hannon's dancing harpsichord quavers in the instrumental passages, lending the song a quaint charm. Keith Farrell's upright bass, combined with Walsh's acoustic guitar, keeps the song in a folk-oriented mode, while Hannon's delectable Mellotron choral, woodwind and string choices enhance its rustic appeal, as does his performance on the zither. The good old Mellotron – one of the mainstays of progressive rock back in the early 1970s – sees something of a welcome revival with this album, adding significantly to the varied tonal colours on display throughout. The final touch to this appealing track is the lovely vocal harmony work by Walsh, Hannon and Matt Lunson that heightens the summery ambience radiating from this song.

'Test Match Special' (Hannon, Walsh)
This tribute to the joys of cricket opens with a series of strange 'boinging' sounds moving from side to side across the stereo picture. These noises are most likely generated by Hannon's Korg synthesiser, and they run into the crunchy, distorted electric guitar riff that powers the song along. Vocals are shared between Hannon, Walsh, Cathy Davey and Matt Lunson, while the lyrics celebrate that feeling of shutting out the rest of the world and totally absorbing oneself in the game at hand – in this case, a five-day 'Test Match Special'. Hannon sounds jubilant, as he settles in the sun with a big TV screen and a cup of Earl Grey tea to become fully in the moment. The sporting action between the two teams is the sole focus here, broken only by 'a streaker, running through the crease' in verse four (cue a wolf-whistle from bassist Keith Farrell). The song eventually dissolves into a manic lead guitar cameo from Tosh Flood, sounding completely unhinged and over-the-top, bringing the song to its conclusion in a welter of guitar feedback.

'The End Of The Over' (Hannon, Walsh)
Piano chords mark out each beat as overlapping voices utter various numbers in repeated countdowns from one to six. The main vocal by Hannon chants variations on 'the end of the over, the over has ended' over a steady but slow crotchet beat, and Walsh joins in until the vocals take on a cod-operatic style. This all eventually resolves into a reprise of the plaintive triple time tune that opened the album on 'The Coin Toss', neatly topping and tailing the album thematically – a device often used in early 1970s progressive rock (a good example being the 1973 Genesis album *Selling England By The Pound*, which

opens and closes with a wistful melodic fragment, much as *The Duckworth Lewis Method* does). It's hugely effective, and as Walsh announces through the vocoder, 'Duckworth and Lewis are out', a similar piano chord to the one, that closed the DC album *Victory For The Comic Muse*, is struck. It neatly wraps up this superb pop album, and as the piano chord fades, ambient sounds of a cricket match in progress, some seagulls and a crowing cockerel play us out.

Bang Goes The Knighthood (2010)

Personnel:
Neil Hannon: vocals, piano, guitar, banjo, keyboards
Thomas Walsh: guest vocals ('The Complete Banker', 'Can You Stand Upon One Leg'), acoustic guitar ('At The Indie Disco', 'The Lost Art Of Conversation')
Cathy Davey: guest vocals ('At The Indie Disco', 'Have You Ever Been In Love', 'Island Life'), drums ('At The Indie Disco')
Tosh Flood: guest vocals ('Down In The Street Below'), electric guitar ('At The Indie Disco')
Simon Little: bass
Tim Weller: drums
Andrew Skeet: orchestral arrangements, conductor (Millennia Ensemble)
Recorded: Exchequer Street Studios, Westland Studios, Dublin. Orchestra recorded at RAK Studios, London between January and April 2009, October 2009 and February 2010
Mixed by Bill Somerville-Large, Guy Massey, Dan Grech-Marguerat (Westland, Beethoven Street and Dragon's Lair Studios, London)
Mastered by Geoff Pesche at Abbey Road Studios, London
Engineers: Fergal Davis, assisted by Ross Martin (Westland); Guy Massey, assisted by Richard Woodcraft (RAK)
Producer: Neil Hannon
Record label: Divine Comedy Records
Released: 31 May 2010
Highest UK chart position: 20

With the completion of *The Duckworth Lewis Method* album, Hannon's attention then turned to a new DC project. With this in mind, he started composing a bunch of songs based around the piano. Recording sessions for this project commenced in January 2009 at Exchequer Studios, Dublin. This studio was operated by composer Brian Crosby and Nick Seymour, bassist with Crowded House. These initial sessions ran through until April, but then, with the imminent release of *The Duckworth Lewis Method* album, Hannon turned his attention to promotional work to support it, which occupied most of the summer. By October, he was free to resume work on the new DC project, which was eventually mixed and mastered by February 2010.

Alongside his work with The Divine Comedy and The Duckworth Lewis Method, Hannon became involved in a series of dramatic works. The first of these was an adaption of Arthur Ransome's novel *Swallows & Amazons*, which had first been published in 1930. Hannon wrote a series of songs to be featured in this drama and the demos for these would eventually be released as a bonus disc with the 2019 DC album *Office Politics*. These demos made for a captivating bonus feature and were mainly just Hannon sitting at his piano singing the songs. As ever, the 15 songs featured contained much humour and some memorable melodies. 'The Black Spot' was one song I found particularly amusing, as Hannon describes the unfortunate things that could happen to someone cursed with the stigma of 'The Black Spot'. One of the other tunes originally written for this drama would appear as 'Island Life' on *Bang Goes The Knighthood*. Performances of the stage musical *Swallows & Amazons* took place at Bristol Old Vic Theatre in 2010, followed by a tour in 2011 and beyond.

While on the subject of Hannon's dramatic works, he had been working with German composer Frank Alva Buecheler since 2009 on an opera project about a child suffering from cancer. In 2011, the music for this new work – now known as *In May* – was described by Hannon as 'really depressing' (as you might expect, dealing with such a morbid subject). The piece was eventually performed in May 2013 at the Lancaster Institute of Contemporary Arts, and in 2016, the music was released as a bonus disc with the DC album *Foreverland*. *In May* harked back, musically, to Hannon's earlier minimalist-influenced, string quartet-based albums *Liberation* and *Promenade*. The *Foreverland* bonus disc featured his vocals, supported by Andrew Skeet (piano), Natalia Bonner (violin), Emil Chakalov (violin), Emma Owens (viola), the ever-present Chris Worsey (cello) and Richard Pryce (double bass). The music was uncompromisingly stark, again showing the influence of Michael Nyman. Some fans loved it, but others were not so keen. However, artistically, it was undeniably another triumph and underlined Hannon's musical flexibility and ambition. The work consisted of 19 short movements, over which Hannon told the grim tale of the young cancer victim's last five months of life. Personally, I found it heavy going, especially after suffering the loss of my own mother to this disease over a similar time period.

A third dramatic work was embarked on, following a Royal Opera House commission. This was based around Leo Tolstoy's *Sevastopol Sketches* and Hannon took three months writing the music for *Sevastopol*, which was supervised by long-time DC collaborator Andrew Skeet and featured regular Divine Comedy contributors Rob Farrer and Chris Worsey. Hannon was not over-enamoured by the final result, though, and this episode appeared to draw a line under his interest in working within the sphere of opera. Audio extracts from *Sevastopol* were subsequently made available on the Royal Opera House website.

The artwork for the new DC album *Bang Goes The Knighthood* is rather fun and features a photo of Hannon – with Sherlock Holmes'-style pipe in his mouth, whilst clad in only a bowler hat and bow tie – taking a foamy bath with his black Labrador dog. The album title is emblazoned above this image. The rear of the CD shows a shocked-looking Hannon at the breakfast table, reading the latest scandal in a newspaper called the *DC Weekly*, which itself has the Hannon-and-dog-in-the-bath photo on its front page.

Bang Goes The Knighthood was released on 31 May 2010, preceded by the single 'At The Indie Disco', which appeared a week earlier. The album saw The Divine Comedy briefly back in the Top 20 of the album charts for the first time since *Regeneration* back in 2001. Amongst the best reviews, Jim Farber in the *NY Daily News* wrote, 'No songwriter alive gets into other people's heads more convincingly', while *Pitchfork* reckoned, 'His days of creating spectacular extravaganzas may be over, but the more modest ambitions on display here are nearly as enjoyable to hear'. Finally, *MusicOMH* assured us: 'Die-hard fans will be pleased the quirky genius is having a good time'.

'Down In The Street Below' (Hannon)
In an album packed with acutely observed character sketches, this song contrasts a love-struck couple in their cosy second-floor apartment, with the hustle and bustle of the masses of humanity milling by in the street below. The opening verse is a scene-setter, as the subject of the song arrives home from work one winter evening for a cosy night in with his partner, to share a meal and watch a movie before settling down in bed together. This verse is set to a rich ballad-style vocal melody, supported by Hannon's piano.

As the scene switches to the next day, the music takes on an urban clamour, with a busy presto rhythm, where the piano is joined by some hectic orchestration. The music brings to life the commotion of a milling throng, as the masses hurry about their business, wrapped up warm against the cold of the season. Hannon observes them as they go about their daily doings in a mad rush.

The music then returns to the relaxing ballad mode that opened the track and finds the protagonist of the song in a high-rise bar 'knocking back mojitos'. As the arrangement builds up to an emotionally charged climax, the subject of the song is questioning the reasons he's doing all the things he does, apparently in the throes of some sort of existential meltdown. As the orchestration swells and Hannon extemporises on the lush melody, it's hard not to be swept up in the impassioned climax of this opening track. The song ends with a brief triple-time fade out of a rapid, repeated piano figure, leading into the burbling sounds of the street.

'The Complete Banker' (Hannon)
Driven by staccato piano chords playing on the beat, this medium-paced song paints a pointed character portrait of an archetypal greedy banker, who evidently 'Caused a second great depression' in his attempts to get even richer by dubious financial manoeuvring. It's a lyric that spears its target mercilessly and is juxtaposed against a jaunty, barrel-house piano accompaniment that gives the track a strong sing-along appeal. The humour disguises a sense of disdain at this reprehensible example of an already rich individual attempting to make himself even wealthier, with scant regard for the effects of his actions on those less fortunate. By the final chorus, the disgraced banker cheerfully admits to being 'a conscience-free, malignant cancer on society', but warns us that if we let our guard down, he'll be back again. There is a tidy but brief

guitar solo on the coda, presumably played by Hannon himself, before a series of staccato, descending piano notes lead to the resounding crash of a reverb-drenched final chord, closing a dramatically theatrical performance.

'Neapolitan Girl' (Hannon)
In a complete change of scene, this next selection transports us back through time to the bombed-out buildings, poverty and squalor of Naples, following the end of the Second World War. The lyric follows the fortunes of a Neapolitan girl, Lola, who has turned to prostitution to survive. This portrait of Lola is tenderly observed in Hannon's lyric, where she is less concerned about right or wrong than where the next meal is coming from. Lola's lovers include clients in both 'the city bank' and 'the British ranks'. Much of the sordid goings-on described here take place behind the headstones in the local cemetery, as Lola struggles to make enough cash to survive.

The music juxtaposed against this lyric is in an upbeat pop styling and has a sing-along catchiness that is contagious, especially the 'Neapolitan girl' chants between the verses. The contrast between the light pop tune and Lola's struggle detailed in the lyrics works surprisingly well, and like many songs on this album, it feels as if it could have come from a theatre production or stage musical, such is the vivid imagery on display.

'Bang Goes The Knighthood' (Hannon)
The piano takes centre stage on this album; in many ways, it's comparable to David Bowie's classic 1971 album *Hunky Dory*, which was similarly built from the piano upwards. Here, Hannon goes for a slow, Germanic-sounding 3/4 rhythm, with a minor-key melody that suits its seedy subject: a sex-obsessed, sadomasochistic politician making frequent visits to a dank London cellar for a rendezvous with a Miss Whiplash-type dominatrix. He lives in fear of a careless word in the wrong ear, then, 'Bang goes the knighthood, the wife and career'. The middle bridge section of the song consists of stabbing piano chords and a vocal melody that crosses the triple time bar lines, making it feel like two time signatures are running against each other. This amplifies the protagonist's outpourings of confused feelings, as he claims that, while being dominated, he at least feels something – preferable to the nothing at all he claims to feel the rest of the time. It's another brilliant character sketch by Hannon – quite vivid in its descriptive detail and disturbingly magnificent.

'At The Indie Disco' (Hannon)
The first single released from the album and unfortunately not a hit, 'At The Indie Disco' is Hannon's tribute to the indie scene of his younger years and is fondly observed. From the regular corner table, beneath 'the poster of Morrissey with a bunch of flowers', to the plea for 'some Blur and some Cure and some Wannadies', it brings to life the essence of the indie scene. The beat is held down by Hannon's partner Cathy Davey, who features on drums

on this track, as well as adding some charming vocals to the mix. DLM's Thomas Walsh throws in some acoustic guitar, while Tosh Flood weighs in on electric guitar. There is a charming, almost homespun feel to this track that I like a lot, and it's spiced up with some sharp orchestration. The best line of the song is: 'She makes my heart beat the same way, as at the start of 'Blue Monday'' – the classic 1983 New Order single, which is, coincidentally, 'Always the last song that they play'.

'Have You Ever Been In Love?' (Hannon)

Here, Hannon makes a more-than-decent tilt at writing a standard. With its lightly swinging beat and dancing piano, this is one of those songs that sum up that lighter-than-air feeling of newly found love. Hannon lists some of the crazy symptoms that can be brought about by falling in love – from dancing in a shopping mall, to suddenly bursting out laughing or feeling as if you can float into the sky – 'like the laws of physics simply don't apply'. This light and airy arrangement fits the subject matter like a glove. Furthermore, the subtly orchestrated instrumental middle passage of the song displays a Bach-like perfection in its ineffable logic, as it flows like a rippling stream down a hillside.

'Assume The Perpendicular' (Hannon)

Marching piano and a crisp military-style snare drum give this track its romping feel, as we're invited out on a trip to one of the stately homes of England. The destination today is the West Country and we're off to Somerset to peruse a stately home 'built in a Georgian style'. The song title goes against 'the horizontal life' and, instead, demands us to rouse ourselves and get up and about, as we do in some style in this song, where we can gawp in wonder at the lintels, architraves and buttresses of the grand old building. Hannon invites one and all to become lords and ladies for a day, as he exclaims with glee, 'Oh, what a gay charade'.

It's a track filled with happiness and good feeling and is quite irresistible. We can revel in the spectacular gardens created by 18th-century gardener Capability Brown, or get lost 'inside the manicured maze', as well as ride for free on 'the ladders round the walls of the circular library' (although this last antic sounds somewhat irresponsible!) – what fun! The track plays on with piano, marching brass, snare drum and Hannon's banjo picking until it's left to peter out naturally. This lends an endearing air of spontaneity to the proceedings, leaving this listener with a smile on his face.

'The Lost Art Of Conversation' (Hannon)

Propelled by rolling piano, this track positively barrels along as Hannon attempts to revive 'The Lost Art Of Conversation'. The verses are crammed with words on countless topics, from actor David Jason and footballer Frank Lampard, to Neolithic tribes in the Pacific, the League of Nations, transubstantiation, Bram Stoker's creation and many more. Like all good conversation, we're reminded that it's going to take time and patience, 'but all the best things do'. A catchy whistling riff is thrown in for good measure and Hannon's driving piano playing, doubled with what sounds like a clavinet later in the track, is a real treat and gives the song its relentless locomotion. There's an amusing verse where one of his comrades attempts to initiate a conversation with 'commuters wearing earphones', and, consequently, suffers from 'conversation hallucinations' – poor chap!

It's a track that is terrific fun to listen to and another very 'up'-sounding performance. In a repeated chorus, we're warned not to try this in public 'or they'll think you've gone insane'. Like many Hannon songs, it uses humour to make a serious point, as in a modern world where many people are plugged into their own media or glued to the screens of their phones, sadly, there seems to be less and less direct person-to-person contact anymore. The song ends with an extended second chorus, as multiple conversations can be heard spread across the stereo sound picture, and these carry on briefly after the music stops.

'Island Life' (Hannon)

This song, transferred from the *Swallows & Amazons* project to feature here, is a vocal duet between Cathy Davey and Neil Hannon and is quite delightful. The long intro nods towards Hannon's interest in minimalism, with its repeated marimba-like hypnotic keyboard riff. The lyrics describe a Utopian existence on a small island and the music sounds suitably tropical. It is a light and airy performance, with Cathy Davey's vocal sounding particularly charming; she has a fragile but lovely tone that is so easy on the ear and it combines beautifully with Hannon's voice, especially when they are harmonising. The mood here is idyllic, and although the song feels light-as-a-feather, it makes for an enchanting interlude, enhancing this album's impressive sense of balance and musical variety. Hannon has few rivals when it comes to rhythmic diversity and melodic/harmonic invention, underlined by the engaging ebb and flow demonstrated on this album.

'When A Man Cries' (Hannon)

The sound of a turning key winding up a musical box opens this track, and as the musical box plays randomly over the opening piano chords, the spell is cast. Providing a clear emotional high point for the album, 'When A Man Cries' is one of Hannon's most finely wrought creations. The first two verses of this deeply penetrating lyric describe the mercurial crying of a child, who is more likely to yell until the hurt is gone, then fall back to relative peace again. In verse three, this is contrasted with an adult man, often borne down with years of emotional baggage and generally tending to suppress feelings of hurt, bottling it all up. This suppression inevitably leads to an explosive release, where 'it's hard to stem the flow' as his 'body shakes, his eyeballs ache, but he doesn't make a sound'.

The perfectly formed middle eight of the song sums up the hopelessness of trying to share the load with a female partner, as she would only try to 'explain it away'. The intensely moving final verse gets to the heart of the matter; as the man 'cries alone', he feels as if he is 'back home, cradled in his mother's arms', and momentarily, 'free from guilt and safe from harm'. When combined with the touchingly beautiful melody and sympathetic orchestration, these lyrics are, for me, some of the most emotionally powerful that Hannon has ever written. Very few songwriters would be capable of matching the perceptive depth Hannon displays on this mini-masterpiece of pristine perfection.

'Can You Stand Upon One Leg?' (Hannon)

We go from the sublime to the ridiculous, especially following such a tenderly emotional song; this is an attempt at out-and-out comedy. That, however, is the essence of Neil Hannon, and this music hall-influenced concoction hits the funny bone with a firm whack! It takes us through a series of challenges that are 'harder than you think', starting with the title challenge of standing on one leg, as Hannon encourages us all to give it a try. The piano plods along amiably and the song's slowly rising melody works well. The next challenge issued is to beat your dad at chess.

A further invitation invites us to 'write a silly song', one that will make everybody sing (just as this one does!), although Hannon concludes, 'It's just like trying to stand on one leg' (in other words, harder than you think). The next dare invites us to 'tell a funny joke' with the grin-inducing add-on: 'One that makes the milk come out your nose'. We then get the opportunity to tell our own funny joke over some staccato rhythmic breaks, complete with sliding whistles, woodblock percussion and other silly noises, to which Hannon encourages us: 'That's not bad, I'm impressed, but here's one, final test'. The finishing challenge is holding a singing note 'for a stupidly long time' and, to make it harder, we need to start 'way up high'. This is the sternest test of all for most of us and Hannon has a definite advantage with his incredible range and voice control. To demonstrate, he closes the song by singing the line, 'Let's see how long you can hold... ', on which he employs his highest vocal range. He proceeds to sustain the word 'hold', with an impressive purity of tone, for an eye-watering 28.9 seconds before closing the song with a short, sweet 'onto a note'. It's funnier the first time you hear it, for sure, but it remains a technically impressive party piece and jolly good fun.

'I Like' (Hannon)

To close the album, Hannon goes for a straightforward, stomping pop tune, selected as a second single release from the album, although it, too, failed to chart. It's a great pop song, though, as Hannon sings the praises of his partner with a host of amusing lyrics to savour, one of the best couplets being: 'I like the way you make me laugh, I like your brain, both left and right half'. Even their pooch receives a name check in the line: 'I like the dog, when he's behaving'. It's a happy love song with a bright beat that, with Hannon's rolling piano and organ chords bolstering it up, is another track with a strong feel-good factor and would and should have brightened up the charts when released as a single in August 2010.

Additional Tracks

'On The Barge' (Hannon)

Appearing as an extra track on the single 'At The Indie Disco', released on 23 May 2010, 'On The Barge' is Hannon's invitation to check out the coolest 'must-go-to' club, taking place on a barge moored on the River Tiber in Rome. Moving along at a moderate shuffle, the verses of this eastern-tinged dance track shamble along pleasantly, lifted by handclaps. Hannon uses his powers of persuasion to encourage his latest potential female dance partner to accompany him to a Friday night of dance-floor grooving, Italian-style. The second section of this song, in which Hannon rhapsodises about how wonderful it will be, is underpinned by Italianate mandolins and a rising melody before a return to the eastern promise of the verse. These two sections play off each other to good effect, and as the coda plays out on an Arabic scale, it feels as if the barge may have become unmoored and started to drift on a journey around the 'boot' of Italy and eastwards towards Turkey, such is the Middle Eastern feel of the music. This is a worthwhile extra track and who could resist an invitation to dance with Mr. Hannon?

'Ya Sumeera' (Hannon)

Released as a download bonus track with *Bang Goes The Knighthood*, this sound collage is a collection of sample loops, the most effective of which is a vintage sample of a female soprano singing the phrase, 'Ya Sumeera'. This is effectively looped in with various synthesised repeating samples of a short duration. The track is constructed in a minimalist manner and its selection of short, repeating sample loops induces a pleasant and rather soothing hypnotic effect.

'The Circular Firing Squad' (Hannon)

Another download bonus track, available with *Bang Goes The Knighthood* on iTunes, this is a sound collage of various sample loops, including some Mellotron chords, synthesiser riffs and piano snippets, shuffled into a random order, with a cajon rhythm entering underneath the sonic mayhem of this experimental piece. It is yet another nod to minimalism, as the changes are slight and gradual, but the overall effect is engaging enough. The title is taken from the lyric of a further download bonus track, 'Napoleon Complex', which will later appear in a more fully arranged form on the 2016 album *Foreverland* – thus, it will be examined in that chapter.

Sticky Wickets (2013)

Personnel:
Neil Hannon: vocals, electric guitar, piano, synthesisers, Vox Continental organ, slide guitar, Farfisa organ, electric piano, zither, melodica, harpsichord, programming, banjo, percussion, string arrangements
Thomas Walsh: vocals, acoustic guitar, drums, percussion, kazoosaphone
Tosh Flood: electric guitar, samples, backing vocals, whistling, Omnichord, mandolin, banjo, piano, percussion
Nick Seymour: bass, whistling, percussion
Tim Weller: drums
Joe Fitzgerald: drums ('Mystery Man')
Neil Finn: additional vocals ('Sticky Wickets')
David Lloyd: spoken word ('Boom Boom Afridi')
Henry Blofeld: spoken word ('It's Just Not Cricket')
Billy Cooper: trumpet ('It's Just Not Cricket', 'The Laughing Cavaliers')
Nelson Bragg: additional percussion ('It's Just Not Cricket')
Daniel Radcliffe: spoken word ('The Third Man')
Cathy Davey: additional vocals ('Line And Length'), backing vocals ('Judd's Paradox')
Stephen Fry: spoken word ('Judd's Paradox')
Matt Berry: spoken word ('Mystery Man')
Andrew Skeet: conductor
Everton Nelson, Lucy Wilkins, Natalie Bonner, Alison Dods, Gillon Cameron, Emil Chakalov: violin
Bruce White, Reiad Chibah, Adrian Smith: viola
Chris Worsey, Ian Burdge, Frank Schaefer: cello
Simon Little, Mary Scully: bass
Isobel Griffiths: contractor, assisted by Lucy Whalley
Recorded at Exchequer Studios, Dublin; additional recording at Play School Studios, Dublin; strings recorded at Snap Studios, London between 6 October 2012 and 3 February 2013
Engineer: Guy Massey (Exchequer and Snap Studios); Neil Hannon (Play School Studios); assistant engineering by Ben McCluskey (Snap Studios)
Mixed by Guy Massey at Fluff Studios, London
Mastered by Geoff Pesche at Abbey Road Studios, London
Producer: Thomas Walsh and Neil Hannon
Record label: Divine Comedy Records
Released: 1 July 2013
Highest UK chart position: 32

In February 2011, Neil Hannon was back in Exchequer Studios, Dublin with Thomas Walsh, working on sessions for the new Pugwash album *The Olympus Sound*, released on 19 August that year. It wasn't until May 2012 that Hannon and Walsh decided to write together for a second Duckworth

Lewis Method release, and initial writing sessions took place at Play School Studios in Dublin during the summer. Demo sessions started on 6 October and continued through the remainder of 2012. DLM moved to Nick Seymour's Exchequer Studios on 21 January 2013 and the Crowded House bass player joined the band for this album. Recording sessions ran through to 3 February, before moving across to Snap Studios in London, where Andrew Skeet conducted Hannon's string arrangements and various guests were called in to overdub their vocal contributions. By April, the new DLM album *Sticky Wickets* had been mastered and the band gathered in May to start rehearsals for touring and promotion. The song 'It's Just Not Cricket' was released as a download single on 9 June and its parent album followed suit on 1 July. DLM then commenced gigs and promotional dates to publicise *Sticky Wickets*.

The front cover artwork features a black and white photo of a streaker – one Michael Angelo, caught in mid-leap above the wicket stumps. The rear of the CD cover was another monochrome photo, this time of Hannon and Walsh in cricket whites on the pitch. Opening up the gatefold design, there are two crotch-level back and front photos, possibly of Hannon, in whites, with a shot of his grassy posterior, and the other a frontal shot where he's handling a cricket ball. The 'Sticky Lyrics' booklet contains some zonked-out-looking photos of the duo, taken in a variety of locations, both looking suitably eccentric – Walsh in a top hat and Hannon in a pith-helmet.

The album garnered much publicity in both music and sporting circles and was, again, well-received. The reviewer for *The Quietus* praised the album: 'While not as instant as their debut, repeated listens definitely provide equal rewards'. Colin Somerville in *The Scotsman* stated, 'These songs capture the essence of British summer like strawberries and cream', while *Get Ready To Rock* weighed in with: 'Music like this deserves to be in every collection'. In terms of sales, *Sticky Wickets* managed a peak of number 32 during its three-week run on the UK album chart.

'Sticky Wickets' (Hannon, Walsh)

The second DLM album opens with a few bars of stabbing staccato organ that sounds as if it's processed through a sequencer. It's joined by some abrasive guitar chords from Neil Hannon that immediately evoke the trademark sound of the Rolling Stones in full raunchy mode. The illusion is completed when the drums, played by Thomas Walsh on this track, make their explosive entrance, with a snare sound that is pure Charlie Watts. Given an added push from an on-the-beat cowbell, it's a fine slice of rock 'n' roll, and as the falsetto vocals arrive, the singing sounds uncannily like the vocal blend of The Who in the 1960s, when Pete Townshend and John Entwistle used to push into their higher vocal ranges. This nigh-on perfect Stones/Who crossover sound gives the album's title track an energising drive. There is a second guitar part courtesy of Tosh Flood, and towards the close of the track, the two guitarists battle it out with rhythmic and lead lines intermingling. Within the mix, Neil

Finn makes a vocal contribution, alongside his Crowded House bandmate Nick Seymour on bass guitar.

The phrase 'Sticky Wicket' is one of those that has come to describe difficult circumstances, but originated in the game of cricket, when the ground around the stumps had become damp and soft, causing the ball to bounce unpredictably. In this song, the lyrics can be read in multiple ways: holding steadfast in a sticky situation, pacing the play in a game of cricket or even as sexual innuendo. It's a fun track and has a pent-up, controlled energy, always sounding like it still has something in the locker. Towards the end of the song, Walsh plays an impressive free-flowing fill around the drum kit, using his tom-toms and snare, and this augments the sense of suppressed power inherent in this recording.

'Boom Boom Afridi' (Hannon, Walsh)

Moving along at a nippy pace in 5/4 time, this celebratory tribute to the Pakistani international cricketer Shahid Afridi (nicknamed 'Boom Boom') delves into a Bhangra influence, with strong eastern-tinged musical themes in the intro/bridge section and thumping percussion, emphasising the 5/4 pulse, in the choruses, where the title is chanted. In cricketing terminology, the mentions of 'flashing hard' in the verses refer to a batsman wielding the bat aggressively and hitting good line and length deliveries indiscriminately. The song moves into full eastern mode during a later instrumental section, with the appearance of sitar and tabla samples and a sliding cello that recalls George Harrison's Indian-influenced tracks on The Beatles' mid-to-late 1960s albums, lending this passage a definite neo-psychedelic flavour. In amongst this eastern-sounding section is an amusing spoken word interlude performed by cricket commentator David Lloyd, where he advises us that if we want to flash, to 'flash 'ard'. A final return to the percussive chorus leads into a dynamic dead-stop ending, closing this fascinating track.

'It's Just Not Cricket' (Hannon, Walsh)

It's back to a music hall influence for this amusing song, released as a download single in advance of the album. The strings slide around whimsical riffs as the verses jog along in a jolly fashion, before the orchestration executes a 'drop through the trapdoor' descent, cueing in choruses that bluster along like a determined power-walker. There are some nifty harmonised electric guitar lines, too, courtesy of Neil Hannon and Tosh Flood, and these loop upwards, while the whistling duo of Tosh Flood and Nick Seymour sound like they're strolling through the mayhem. Thomas Walsh sings the verses and the choruses are sung by Hannon, the second of which is multi-tracked and harmonised by him, supported solely by handclaps – an effective arrangement touch.

The lyrics comment on unfair and unjust practises in sport, such as ball-tampering, performance-enhancing drugs and awards of huge bonuses, berating that it's just not cricket, chaps! It's all terrific fun and best of all is the spoken word contribution by cricket commentator Henry 'Blowers' Blofeld, as his plummy accent throws in some rib-tickling comments throughout the song. For this recording, Thomas Walsh inducted one of his relations into the band in the shape of percussionist Nelson Bragg, who was also part of Beach Boy Brian Wilson's concurrent line-up. The song also stars trumpeter Billy Cooper, best known for his association with the Barmy Army, who follow the England cricket team around the globe, providing musical accompaniment.

'The Umpire' (Hannon, Walsh)
The mood turns to one of poignancy for this sad ode, dedicated to the umpires and referees of the world, struggling as they do to uphold their dignity in this technology-driven age. Hannon's staccato piano quavers give the track its slow, forward motion, as he takes on the character of the underappreciated umpire, who has 'egg and soldiers' for his breakfast and attempts to 'avoid the news' before heading out in his Ford Escort, as the Jags and Ferraris leave him in their wake once more. Hannon takes the main vocal and ponders, 'Who would aspire to be an umpire?', when every decision they make is open to being called into question, following video replays and the like. It's a sympathetic portrait and it's this kind of track that contrasts with the jollier songs, giving this album a perfect balance. The umpire in question just wants to get away from it all, wondering if he'd be missed if he took a holiday.

The music carries a good deal of pathos, with its minor key ambience, and as the chorus comes in, there is a deep-toned drone sounding like a bass voice, but more likely generated by the 1980s electronic instrument, the Omnichord, which Tosh Flood plays on this track. This sound imparts an almost ghostly atmosphere to the choruses. The backing vocal harmony work is cleverly done, and towards the end, we hear a repeated and somewhat creepy-sounding chant of 'Que existo arbitrum' (arbitrum refers to synchronised digital technology and 'que existo' translates as 'I exist' in Spanish). It is no wonder that the final chorus warns us that sport is turning into 'a computer game', with the poor old umpire becoming 'Just a relic of yesterday'. In a perfect final twist to this moving song, a repeating, looped, female voice enters, whispering, 'Umpires don't cry' – a clear nod to the classic 1975 hit single 'I'm Not In Love' by 10cc (which featured the loop, 'Big boys don't cry').

'Third Man' (Hannon, Walsh)
If you didn't know better, you might mistake this track for a 1970s ELO outtake, such is its uncanny resemblance to the sound of Jeff Lynne and his crew in their heyday. The choppy string arrangement is pure ELO and the shouts of 'Hey, hey' sound like the ELO main man himself! It's a fine pop song that nods to both the cricketing term 'Third Man' and the 1949 film noir

of the same name, starring Orson Welles. In cricket, the third man is a fielding position behind the wicketkeeper on the off-side, at around 45 degrees to the wicket and out towards the boundary.

Thomas Walsh takes the lead vocal duties on this song and is relegated to cricketing duty as 'Third Man', but admits in the chorus, 'I daydream away down at third man'. He sounds a bit distracted out in the field, as, away from most of the action, his fantasies roam to planning crimes 'like Harry Lime' (from the film *The Third Man*). There is some nifty wordplay on display, and after the second chorus, the song morphs unexpectedly into a moody snippet of Anton Karas' theme to *The Third Man*, also known as 'The Harry Lime Theme'. In this brief section, there is a spoken word contribution by *Harry Potter* actor Daniel Radcliffe. His words sum up the absentminded daydreams Walsh is experiencing on the cricket pitch, as he ponders: 'Am I in a field in England or in the dark streets of Vienna?'

After this curious interlude, we are back with the ELO flavour; after a few more chants of 'Hey, hey', the string section embarks on a bracing coda, laced with up and down chromatic string runs, before closing elegantly with some piano arpeggios.

'Chin Music' (Hannon, Walsh)

This triple-time instrumental is named after the cricketing term of the same name. It is a bowling strategy in cricket, in which a short-pitched delivery, bouncing once, then reaches the batsman at head height.

Employing assorted percussion galore, this performance evinces a strong fairground ambience, with crisp snare drum to the fore. It sports a delightful bounce, as Hannon's harpsichord, melodica and zither combine with Tosh Flood's mandolin to give 'Chin Music' a distinctive 'merry-go-round' flavour, resulting in a scintillating instrumental interlude, the fairground illusion magnified by some thumping timpani drums.

'Out In The Middle' (Hannon, Walsh)

The laid-back AOR groove on display in this soft-rock ballad recalls the style of 1970s band Ace; their vocalist, Paul Carrack, would be well-suited to this song. The vocals are augmented by processed backing harmonies, with liberal use of autotune. Despite my usual aversion to vocals processed in this way, in this case, it works pretty well and is, thankfully, employed with a modicum of good taste.

Thomas Walsh's casually strummed acoustic guitar is supported by some economical high-octave licks from Tosh Flood's electric guitar, while Hannon's electric piano chords add to the lightness of touch of the performance. Walsh sings lead on the verses, while Hannon takes over on the choruses. The AOR flow of the song is oddly disrupted by a short Hannon piano excursion into 5/4 time, although this section, agreeable as it is, doesn't really go anywhere in particular. We are soon returned to the song's mellow groove for a short but neat guitar solo from Tosh Flood, before a slow fade-out soaked in processed vocal harmonies.

The song title may be a reference to the batting order in cricket, where, if you are in the middle, you would be between positions four and seven. The lyrics can also be read as referring to testing one's mettle and facing up to your fears.

'Line And Length' (Hannon, Walsh)

We move into funk territory with this percussively driven creation, based around a programmed drum rhythm. Neil Hannon and Tosh Flood serve up some funky rhythm guitar playing, which, in combination with the soulful backing vocals from Hannon, Walsh, Flood and Cathy Davey, make this track sound uncannily like mid-1980s Scritti Politti.

Hannon raps over this backing, giving us a lesson in cricket ball aerodynamics and bowling technique, as he expounds on the technical terms of 'Line And Length'. The first verse elucidates the line of the delivery of a cricket ball: the direction of its trajectory, measured through the horizontal axis. The backing vocal chants of 'Check your line and length/Shoulda, woulda, coulda' give this track an irresistible catchiness. Verse two tackles the 'length' parameter: the length of the delivery being how far down the pitch the ball bounces. Cathy Davey adds a later rap section which expands on the subject of getting the ball where it ought to be: 'In the corridor of uncertainty'. It's all very technical and a most unusual rap, starkly in contrast to the predictability of most records that inhabit that genre of music. As an added bonus, Hannon follows this section with a brief synthesiser solo that sounds straight out of early-1970s progressive rock a la Rick Wakeman – tasty!

'The Laughing Cavaliers' (Hannon, Walsh)

The *joie de vivre* radiated by this album is contagious, as the drunken-sounding slow march of this good-humoured song proves. Some crisp snare rolls from Tim Weller combine with Hannon's honky-tonk piano, Tosh Flood's banjo and the trumpet of Billy Cooper for this cacophonous but celebratory drinking song for amateur cricketers. Musically, it is close in feel to 'You're A Good Man, Albert Brown' from the 1987 Dukes of Stratosphear album *Psonic Psunspot* – a song similarly driven by bar-room piano and a boozy atmosphere.

There are amusing couplets a-plenty here (try: 'When the world is wobbling, we're stoic and we're steady/They will sing about us when we're dead-y') and Hannon and Walsh are joined vocally by The Theatrical Cavaliers – members of a cricket club of the same name based around Dublin. Their raucous vocalising certainly adds to the inebriated air of this short but fun-filled performance.

'Judd's Paradox' (Hannon, Walsh)

In complete contrast to the previous track, 'Judd's Paradox' introduces a more serious note into the proceedings via a wonderfully poetic reflection on the origins of the game of cricket, addressing the class divisions inherent in its gestation. The spoken word verses are narrated by Stephen Fry, his voice carrying a fair degree of gravitas, despite the subtle humour on display in the lyrics.

Musically, the track leans towards the epic in places but with exquisite attention to dynamics. Fry's spoken verses are supported by two seesawing guitar notes and a gorgeous cello arrangement that imparts a classical grace, giving a perfect balance between music and narration. Thomas Walsh sings lead on the choruses, with Neil Hannon on backing response vocals, as the pair ponder, 'How could it be, colonial brains conceived, that glorious game' – therein lies the paradox under examination in this song.

A grand, orchestrated central passage takes the song close to classic progressive rock-territory, as violin, cello and tubular bells are employed to evoke a grandiose splendour, close to the style of Russian composer Sergei Prokofiev. Towards the end of this passage, Hannon's guitar emits a subtle burst of perfectly controlled, deep-toned, throbbing feedback beneath the glowing string arrangement. The track then takes a dynamic dip back to the seesawing guitar notes and resonant cello for its final Stephen Fry-intoned verse.

In this last spoken interlude, the wit and wisdom of the lyrics combine profundity with humour, as he intones, 'The bourgeoisie bat, the proletariat, toil in the fields all day', then admits that, although he should be incensed by this fact, cricket is still 'a damn good game'. Pondering on the peasants revolting against such oppression, he hopes that if they decide to 'storm the pavilions', it can take place 'after the afternoon session'! The final choruses feature some beautiful harmony singing, as Hannon and Walsh's voices are enhanced by those of Cathy Davey and Tosh Flood. A final brushstroke is provided by the accompaniment of some casually picked banjo notes, courtesy of Hannon, followed by dovetailing cello lines and a portentous crash on a gong, closing one of the highlights of the album.

'Mystery Man' (Hannon, Walsh)

This boogie-like invention sees a return to light-hearted tomfoolery, as stride piano and a walking bass line propel the whole caboodle along, while Walsh provides a touch of kazoosaphone and Hannon riffs away on a Vox Continental organ – an instrument that adds a key ingredient to the strolling feel of this recording.

The 'Mystery Man' in question is the unpredictable cricketer, who leaves the opposition in a fluster with his 'Wrist spin, top spin, leg spin, off spin' and his 'In-swinger, out-swinger, shake-it-all-about-swinger'. It's definitely the kind of song that could have you dancing around the room (if that's your thing!), such is its rhythmic forward thrust. It briefly moves into a bolero rhythm at one point and there is a concise rockabilly-style guitar solo by Tosh Flood that is a model of economy.

Matt Berry steps up towards the end to provide us with an update on the scores at the end of the second day's play, as he amusingly broadcasts the action in an imaginary match between the band members and a combined team of notable cricketers. The band boogies on in the background, and in an amusing ending, his last pronouncement is, 'G. M. Massey: 0. Trod on wicket', as the song ends with a minor-major ninth – a variation on Vic Flick's famous 'James Bond chord'.

'Nudging And Nurdling' (Hannon, Walsh)

The closing track on *Sticky Wickets* gives practically the entire cast a chance to join in, along with a sprinkling of celebrity pals, as all and sundry get a chance to speak the words 'nudging' and 'nurdling' in whatever silly voices they wish. Based on a nagging, insistent riff, mostly played on various keyboards over a medium-tempo rhythm section, this closing salvo is, in truth, something of a filler track. It is initially amusing, but less so on repeated listens. The assembled cast sound as if they are having a good time, though, and it all climaxes in a chaotic ending, bringing to a close this good-humoured and generally fun-packed album. Its complementary brace of more poignant tunes ('The Umpire' and 'Judd's Paradox') results in a perfect balance of quality material.

For the record, 'nurdling' is a cricketing term for scoring runs by using low-risk shots to gently nudge the ball into vacant areas of the field.

Foreverland (2016)

Personnel:
Neil Hannon: vocals, acoustic guitar, electric guitar, piano, mandolin, banjo, keyboards, zither, harmonica; percussion, bass, drums (last three on 'Napoleon Complex' and 'How Can You Leave Me On My Own')
Andrew Skeet: piano, conducting, orchestration
Ian Watson: accordion
Rob Farrer: percussion
Simon Little: bass, backing vocals, handclaps
Tim Weller: drums
Celine Saout: harp
Jake Jackson: backing vocals, handclaps, whistling ('Funny Peculiar')
David Jackson: penny whistle ('Foreverland')
Billy Cooper: piccolo trumpet ('To The Rescue')
Rosie Jenkins: oboe ('How Can You Leave Me On My Own')
Cathy Davey: vocals, backing vocals ('Funny Peculiar' and 'Napoleon Complex')
String Squadron:
Adrian Smith, Alison Dods, Bruce White, Chris Worsey, Emma Owens, Everton Nelson, Frank Schaefer, Gillon Cameron, Ian Burdge, Ian Humphries, Lucy Wilkins, Matt Ward, Patrick Kiernan, Pete Hanson, Reiad Chibah, Richard George, Richard Pryce, Rick Koster, Simon Baggs, Steve Morris, Tom Pigott-Smith and Warren Zielinski
Brass Division:
Billy Cooper, John Ryan, Mark Templeton, Matt Gunner, Richard Edwards, Richard Watkins, Sebastian Philpott and Trevor Mires
Woodwind Corps:
Eliza Marshall, Martin Robertson, Richard Skinner and Rosie Jenkins
Nathan Klein: additional orchestration
Orchestra contractor: Isobel Griffiths, assisted by Lucy Whalley
Recorded at Master Chord Studios and AIR (London) Studios; National Concert Hall, Dublin; At Home in The Sticks between 20 September 2015 and 3 February 2016
Engineer: Jake Jackson, assisted by Michele G. Catri (Master Chord), Fiona Cruickshank and John Prestage (AIR)
Producer: Neil Hannon
Record label: Divine Comedy Records
Released: 2 September 2016
Highest UK chart position: 7

In the period between 2011 and 2013, Neil Hannon became involved with various Irish animal charities, particularly Dogs In Distress, for whom he and Cathy Davey performed various benefit gigs. There was also a new charity co-founded by Davey, along with Martina and Deborah Kenny: My Lovely Horse Rescue. The latter was named after Hannon's humorous song 'My Lovely

Horse', written for the *Father Ted* series back in the early 1990s. In 2014, the couple moved to Kildare to be closer to this horse rescue centre.

During the first few months of 2015, Hannon, again, played on sessions for Pugwash, this time for their latest album, *Play This Intimately (As If Among Friends)*, which featured guest appearances from Jeff Lynne, Ray Davies and Andy Partridge. There were also some performances at summer festivals by The Divine Comedy, this time with the line-up of Hannon (guitar, vocals), Andrew Skeet (keyboards), Ian Watson (accordion), Simon Little (bass) and Tim Weller (drums). On 20 September, Neil Hannon and Andrew Skeet, along with sound engineer Jake Jackson, initiated sessions for a new DC project at Master Chord Studios, London. These sessions continued through September, then moved to AIR (London) Studios into October to record the orchestral parts. The new DC album *Foreverland* was mixed by 3 February 2016.

The summer brought some sad news when, on 17 June, The Divine Comedy's former drummer Miggy Barradas suffered a fatal heart attack at only 50 years of age. The death of David Bowie earlier in 2016 had also shocked and saddened Hannon, and he was subsequently invited to perform at the David Bowie Prom at the Royal Albert Hall on 29 July, at which he sang two Bowie songs: 'Station To Station' and 'This Is Not America'.

The new album was preceded by two digital single releases: 'Catherine The Great' on 24 June and 'How Can You Leave Me On My Own' on 26 August, neither of which troubled the charts, despite their exceptional quality. The parent album was released on 2 September and the burst of initial sales to the faithful shot it into the album chart at number seven during September, the highest chart placing for a DC album since 1999.

The album artwork displays a painting of a rather regal-looking lady leaning on a globe with radiance emitting from it. To either side of her are scenes of ships, aeroplanes, an airship and the Statue of Liberty, overlooked by some mounted camels on a quayside and a row of old-time dancing girls along the bottom of the scene. The painting is rendered in deep reds, greens and yellows and looks quite striking, overlaid as it is with the words 'The Divine Comedy' in creamy yellow handwriting. The rear has the album title displayed at the top and a track listing. In the fold-out cover, there are photos of Neil Hannon in a militaristic-looking uniform, along with his partner Cathy Davey looking beautiful in a sheer, long-flowing dress and headgear. They look every inch the perfect couple, although Hannon is sporting a rather serious-looking countenance in the photos.

Foreverland proved to be Hannon's most lushly orchestrated work since *Absent Friends* in 2004 and was generally well-received at the time. Dan Kok at *Pop Matters* praised the album as 'Fresh and impressively in tune with the rest of the musical landscape', *Richer Sounds* called it 'The consummate Divine Comedy album... one of the albums of the year' and Michael Smith at *Renowned For Sound* reckoned: 'The album's finer points are perfectly crafted... *Foreverland* comes off as another stellar release'.

'Napoleon Complex' (Hannon)
Swirling string lines announce the arrival of the 11th DC studio album, introducing a song that first appeared in demo form back in 2010 as a bonus download track with *Bang Goes The Knighthood,* although there were a few lyrical revisions made before this glorious definitive version was recorded. The intro and choruses are built on three ascending, then descending, piano chords accompanied by tubular bell strikes, as the distinctive and charming voice of Cathy Davey chants the song title. The clever arrangement builds up a degree of tension in the music, which lends it a poised-on-the-edge feel. This is achieved by a combination of Hannon's piano, banjo and canny use of various percussion instruments. These are judiciously deployed and panned across the stereo spectrum, giving the track a nice sense of space for the lyrics to occupy.

It's a song dedicated to anyone who is vertically challenged and refers to that old chestnut about short folks compensating for their lack of stature by performing demonstrative deeds and is, of course, named after that notorious French emperor Napoleon Bonaparte. As usual, there are some sharp couplets in the lyrics and the occasional sound effect to enhance certain lines. My personal favourite accompanies the couplet: 'Who was the true inventor of the infamous circular firing squad', followed by a command to fire and the sound of said firing squad discharging their rifles. It feels as if the gunfire is moving around the listener – a very effective use of panning, if slightly alarming! The lyrics in the second verse of the demo version had included a mention of Margaret Thatcher, but this is changed here to the 'Child Catcher' in reference to a character from the 1968 film *Chitty Chitty Bang Bang*, played by actor Robert Helpmann.

As with many tracks on *Foreverland*, the orchestration is superb, as the string section plays chromatic slides between the lines of the verses, displaying the ongoing ELO influence on Hannon's muse. A combination of strings and choral effects lend the track a grandiose splendour and it closes by winding down to just Hannon's banjo picking and tubular bells, following the up and down piano chords on the choruses.

'Foreverland' (Hannon)
The album's title track opens with the evocative sound of an old sailing ship's creaking timbers as we are mentally transported to the deck of said vessel, scanning the horizon with our telescope in search of a glimpse of this mythical paradise. The assembled crew chant, 'What are we looking for?', cueing in Neil Hannon's lyric, which presents us with a vision of that long-sought Utopia – the mysterious, seemingly unobtainable, Shangri-La, Nirvana, Heaven – call it what you will. The setting of this particular Utopian destination is the perfect island, shrouded in mist and with 'a tropical breeze, blowing through the palm trees' as 'Birds of Paradise fly'. There's something so moving about the yearning expressed in this song, along with a deep

sense of desperation. The storyline of the crew of a sailing ship seeking a perfect Utopia is, for me, analogous to the human race. We are on our own 'spaceship Earth' voyaging across the cosmic ocean through time and space in the somewhat vain hope that, someday, we may arrive at a better, more peaceful future place and time than the present day. Pure fantasy for sure, but this song touches me deeply in some profound way. Lyrically, it seems to have a clear link with Hannon's *Swallows and Amazons* project, and also shares something with the great psychedelic-era trend of songwriters looking back to childhood innocence for inspiration. Such can be heard in certain late-1960s compositions by artists like Syd Barrett, The Beatles, The Incredible String Band and The Small Faces.

Musically, it is given a distinctive flavour by the accordion playing of Ian Watson and a contribution on penny whistle from Dave Jackson (ex-Van der Graaf Generator), whose son Jake engineered the album. Jackson's keening penny whistle adds greatly to the sense of yearning inherent in this song, and there is some lovely orchestration supporting this wistful melody, too. Florid piano runs from Andrew Skeet also enhance the unique atmosphere conjured up here and this arrangement presents a cornucopia of sonic delights, creating the illusion of a tropical island idyll. Hannon's vocal is heartfelt and wonderfully expressive. As he sings the lines, 'I know that the crew are dying of hunger/But I'm sure it can't take much longer', it conjures that feeling of 'hanging on in quiet desperation', as expressed many years ago by Roger Waters on 'Time' from the Pink Floyd album *Dark Side Of The Moon*. As the music ends, we return to the sound of a creaking ship's timbers once more, as the voyage of hope continues.

'Catherine The Great' (Hannon)

Opening with a harp glissando and grand, brass-laden orchestration acting as a kind of fanfare, 'Catherine The Great' is a DC classic from the word go. Pushed as the lead-off download single, it was available in advance of the album. This glorious mid-tempo pop tune moves along smartly, enhanced by a tumbling harpsichord line with authentic shakes thrown in, giving the track an undertow of classicism that swirls beneath the drive of the catchy vocal melody.

Hannon's lyrics deal with the phenomenon of infatuation with a historical figure – in this case, the 18th-century Empress of Russia, Catherine II. The song is a virtual love letter to Her Majesty, as Hannon pines: 'She looked so bloody good on a horse'. There are several examples of his off-the-wall lyrical dexterity on display here and few other lyricists would've come up with a rhyme like: 'There were few brainier/Just ask the King of Lithuania'. One suspects that the outpouring of passion in this song could also be revealing Hannon's feelings for his romantic partner, Cathy Davey. This is especially accurate, as, in the *Foreverland* booklet and CD artwork, there are some gorgeous photos in which she is dressed up rather regally – one of them posing with a merry-go-round horse and looking every inch like a modern 'Catherine The Great'!

The middle section of the song explodes into an impressively big, bold, brass-driven descending sequence. This comes to a hammering staccato conclusion as the orchestral intro passage returns once more, but this time accompanied by deep-toned, bass voices holding the root notes while a choir chant: 'Yakaterina Alexeyevna' (the Russian moniker of the Empress). It all sounds rather grand and very Russian. It is followed by a superb mandolin solo from Hannon that sits beautifully with the track, as it plays subtle variations on the verse melody.

The concluding verse slowly winds down, as Hannon, in his fantasies about the Russian empress, yearns to be able to 'tell her a joke' or 'bake her a cake', despite the temporal gulf between them. This is a similar dilemma to that of the protagonist of The Who's 1967 single 'Pictures Of Lily', where a 1960s lad becomes infatuated with a 1920s pin-up girl via pictures of her.

'Funny Peculiar' (Hannon)
With its gently loping offbeat guitar strokes, this light-hearted confection is performed as a duet between Neil Hannon and Cathy Davey, who take turns to declare their own 'Funny Peculiar' endearments to each other. It's a charming performance by the duo, interspersed with a catchy piano riff. The whistling solo in the central passage is performed by studio engineer Jake Jackson. It is shadowed by an identical piano line and includes a nifty chromatic rise that will test your whistling skills, should you attempt to whistle along with it! We are pretty much in MOR territory here, but, like most things he turns his hand to, Hannon does it so well that the effect is one of pure delight.

'The Pact' (Hannon)
On the subject of solidarity and brotherhood, this stirring triple-time song invites us to 'man the barricades together'. The intro sequence recalls that of the Mike Rutherford song 'Your Own Special Way', a minor hit for Genesis in 1977. Hannon's entreaty to an Entente Cordiale highlights his Francophile leanings – a consistent thread throughout the career of The Divine Comedy and a possible reason for his music's particular popularity in France. Ian Watson's accordion arpeggios accentuate the Gallic feel on display and imbue the song with a distinctive essence, while the tasteful orchestration supports its waltz-like flow.

'To The Rescue' (Hannon)
Many songs on *Foreverland* reflect Neil Hannon's life and activities with Cathy Davey, and this one in particular feels like it could be dedicated to Davey's My Lovely Horse Rescue charity. Having said that, the song functions perfectly well in a broader context as an update on the 'noble knight riding to

the rescue' scenario and is inspiring and uplifting for that reason. There is a good deal of positivity on this album, and this song is a great example of the good vibes that resonate through much of *Foreverland*.

Musically, the tempo is medium-slow, with a Spartan rhythm guitar playing a figure every couple of bars, as eddying strings swirl like whirlpools under the choruses. The best arrangement touch of all, however, is Billy Cooper's fluttering trumpet solo on the coda, which manages to blend pathos with celebration in a sense of unerring rightness and is a clear highlight of the track and of the album – lovely!

'How Can You Leave Me On My Own' (Hannon)

This track opens with a series of strange noises which sound like a cross between someone riding a rusty tricycle in need of oiling and a hungry seal at feeding time! Hannon's stomping piano storms this track along as the thumping drums keep up with his energetic keyboard pummelling. It's almost a rock 'n' roll performance, with some 1950s-style rock piano thrown in as it proceeds.

It seems that, without his other half to balance him out, Hannon reverts back to a bachelor lifestyle, as he devolves from 'a beer-swilling, time-killing moron' in the first verse to 'a bad smelling, couch dwelling dickhead' in the second. He consumes 'too many cups of tea' and 'too many biscuits', and even admits, 'I look at naked ladies, 'cause I'm too weak to resist it'. Released on 26 August as the second download single from the album, it once again didn't trouble the charts, excellent though it was. Hannon's vocals are full of character, employing both his mid and bass range. There is an amusing arrangement touch at the end of one of the choruses when he changes the title chant to 'How can you leave me on my...oboe', cueing in a lively solo on said instrument, courtesy of Rosie Jenkins. After a final chorus, the track ends with the rusty tricycle/seal noises that it began with, closing a track that is both energetic and fun.

'I Joined The Foreign Legion (To Forget)' (Hannon)

The sound of applause ushers in a supper-club piano, accompanied by rustling and an occasional cough from the audience. The piano previews the song's melody, with a distinct cabaret feel. It is yet another song with a French connection. The band take over, providing the casually jogging, slow rhythm of this mildly amusing number. Hannon's lead vocal is supported by backing vocals that chant the first five words of the title in response to his crooning and there is a judicious use of choral effects as the song's gentle dynamic rises and falls like slow waves. For me, the lyrics bring to mind the 1931 Laurel & Hardy film *Beau Chumps*, where Oliver Hardy, in an attempt to forget his unfaithful lover (Jean Harlow), coerces Stan Laurel into joining the Foreign Legion with him. The magnificent Charles Middleton plays the garrison commandant, delivering this memorable line after one of Stan

Laurel's episodes of confusion: 'You forgot what you came here to forget? – well, I'll see to it that you don't forget what you're here for!'

In this song, Neil Hannon is obviously hoping for a similar loss of memory in the hope of forgetting a former lover, best enshrined in the priceless couplet: 'She said I'd find it easier/If I had amnesia'. It seems to have worked, as he then admits: 'Who she was I cannot recollect'. Another notable musical feature is Hannon's casual but plaintive harmonica contribution, enhancing a track that comes across as a pleasant diversion, rather than a major statement.

'My Happy Place' (Hannon)

In this song, we are accompanying Hannon on a further quest in search of that elusive longed-for place, where peace of mind rules over the usual difficulties of life: in effect, his 'happy place'. Most of us have one of these, in either a physical or a mental manifestation. It's a song that moves from tension to tranquillity and back again several times. As Hannon sings of a place where 'the mountains rise on either side of a peaceful valley', we are, again, mentally whisked away to the serenity of a location where 'a gentle breeze blows through the trees' to ease our troubled mind. By the final verse, his dilemma is the constant possibility that a perfect life with the one he loves 'could all be snatched away', posing the question: 'Where would I go, when you're my happy place?'

The musical arrangement brings in violin and cello, along with Hannon's favoured banjo – an instrument that is featured heavily on much of his later output, including much of this album.

'A Desperate Man' (Hannon)

This exciting track employs a simple piano riff set to a Latin beat with assorted percussion driving it forward. It sports a perfectly judged arrangement that builds from the piano and percussion intro, gradually introducing more instrumentation as it powers along, until, finally, it has a full orchestra with strings and blaring brass reinforcing its simple but earnest chord structure. The Latin rhythm works in combination with a more Slavic feel via the Middle Eastern scale employed. This is especially prevalent in the instrumental break, which sounds remarkably like it's played on an Asian double-reed woodwind instrument called a shehnai. Some chromatic up-and-down piano runs also add a feeling of desperation and tension to the music.

Lyrically, it follows a fugitive of some kind and the song has a breathless, running feel that is genuinely exhilarating to listen to. The protagonist of the song initially adopts the disguise of a nun to make his escape, steals a paper – only to see his picture in it, begs food from a farmer's daughter and sleeps between the truckers on an overnight ferry – all to get back to the object of his affections. Whether he is obsessed, is going against a restraining order to stay away or is innocent and has been framed is never revealed, but the result is a tensely thrilling song that enlivens the second half of the album. You could well imagine this track being used as theme music for a dramatic TV action thriller.

'Other People' (Hannon)
This brief song dispenses the wise dictum of respecting the fact that whoever your life partner may be, they have inevitably had a life before meeting you. It points out the fact that without their previous liaisons with other people, they would probably not be quite the same person they are today. A philosophical middle eight goes on to invoke the cosmic perspective on day-to-day life 'when set against eternity', and warns against that green-eyed monster – jealousy – deeming it 'worthless and destructive, and always counter-productive'. The major surprise comes in the third verse of this string-buoyed ballad, in which Hannon's lyrics peter out unexpectedly with the line, 'and, um, blah, blah, blah', as if he has said all he wanted to say on the subject at this point in the song.

'The One Who Loves You' (Hannon)
This is a lovely song – it moves forward at a stately pace, riding atop a repeated, cyclical riff played by the string section, underpinned by timpani beats marking out time every few bars. This gives it a slow build and ample room for Neil Hannon to express himself lyrically, giving this paean to love its considerable grace and posture. The choruses are truly ecstatic, rising and falling as they do in chromatic fashion, with a delightful spread of chords supporting the simple but emotive melody. As the song progresses, the orchestration becomes more elaborate and the key modulates up a tone for each new verse, giving the track a sense of intensifying passion.

The lyrics reflect on the difficulties inherent in finding a truly compatible life partner and how special it is if/when you finally do. As usual, Hannon's wit and wisdom shine through in equal proportions with some deft lyrical touches. In the second verse, he equates the likelihood of discovering the perfect partner as 'like finding the lesser-spotted dodo, in Soho... so rare'. The bottom line in this song, one feels, is that Hannon is absolutely certain that he has found the girl of his dreams – this is clearly a love song to his partner Cathy Davey. His final verdict on the long and difficult search to find true love is a triumphant: 'It's worth it – it's really, really worth it'. Providing a perfect ending to one of my own personal favourite Divine Comedy albums, this sublime love song is, for me, up there with Hannon's finest creations.

Office Politics (2019)

Personnel:
Neil Hannon: vocals, Gretsh electric guitar, Rickenbacker bass, piano, percussion, Roland JV-1080, Sequential Circuits Prophet 5, Novation Mini-Nova, Mellotron, Korg Volca Beats, Korg SV-1, Fender Jazzmaster electric guitar, drums, Solina String Ensemble, Arturia Oberheim SEM, mandolin, glockenspiel, Vacuum Plug-in, GEM Jumbo 61 R-6, Jumbo organ, Percy Faith cut-ups, harmonica, Yamaha Portasound PSS-170, Arturia iMini, Korg Monotron Delay, Burns electric guitar, Resonator acoustic guitar, Vox Continental Plug-in, banjo, Martin acoustic guitar, handclaps
Tosh Flood: Fender Telecaster electric guitar, Epiphone Texan acoustic guitar, Epiphone 12-string acoustic guitar, Gibson SG electric guitar, Gibson Les Paul electric guitar, backing vocals, Eastwood Baritone electric guitar, Rickenbacker 330 electric guitar, Arturia CS-80 V3, Mini-Nova, Novo electric guitar, Omnichord, Epiphone Eldorado acoustic guitar, handclaps, drums
Ian Watson: Prophet 5, Lira Finger 5 organ, accordion, Jumbo organ, Mellotron, handclaps, backing vocals
Andrew Skeet: piano, Wurlitzer, whistling, Roland Juno-60, handclaps, backing vocals, additional orchestration, conducting
Simon Little: Fender bass, Hofner bass, Warwick bass, Korg Volca bass, sound effects, handclaps, backing vocals
Tim Weller: drums, percussion, handclaps, Roland 808 drum machine
Ber Quinn: backing vocals
Pete Ruotolo: backing vocals
Sonia Jones, Hazel Fernandez, Kate Lissoon: backing vocals
Chris Difford, Cathy Davey, Thomas Walsh: backing vocals ('Absolutely Obsolete')
Warren Zielinski, Richard George, Alison Dods, Patrick Kiernan, Tom Pigott-Smith, Natalia Bonner, Lucy Wilkins, Perry Montague-Mason, Gillon Cameron: violin
Bruce White, Emma Owens, Reiad Chibah: viola
Chris Worsey, Caroline Dale, Ian Burdge: cello
Richard Pryce: bass
David Pyatt, John Ryan: French horn
Mark Templeton, Richard Edwards: trombone
Dan Newell: trumpet
Owen Slade: tuba
Richard Skinner: bassoon
Eliza Marshall: flute
Max Spiers: oboe
Martin Robertson: clarinet
Orchestra contracted by Lucy Whalley
Recorded at The Menagerie, Kildare; Herbert Place and Sonic Studios, Dublin; AIR (London) Studios; Snap Studios, London; Fluff Studios, London between September 2017 and October 2018

Engineers: Ber Quinn, assisted by Kevin Callanan (Menagerie); Ber Quinn (Herbert Place); Jake Jackson, assisted by John Prestage (AIR); Guy Massey, assisted by Tom Leach (Snap); Guy Massey (Fluff)
Mastered by Frank Arkwright at Abbey Road Studios, London
Producer: Neil Hannon
Record label: Divine Comedy Records
Released: 7 June 2019
Highest UK chart position: 5

To promote the release of *Foreverland* in September 2016, The Divine Comedy rehearsed with a line-up of Neil Hannon (vocals, guitar), Andrew Skeet (keyboards), John Evans (guitar) – later replaced by Tosh Flood on his return from touring with Pugwash, Ian Watson (accordion), Simon Little (bass) and Tim Weller (drums). Following a final rehearsal in London in October, the band embarked on an extensive UK and European tour, extending through to March 2017. Recordings from this tour later appeared on the live album *Loose Canon*, which was initially available by mail order or from the DC merchandising stall but was given a full release in 2018.

In September 2017, the band decamped to Ireland and began recording sessions at Hannon's own studio, The Menagerie in Kildare. Following these initial sessions, Andrew Skeet oversaw orchestral overdubs for the new album at AIR (London) Studios at the end of October. Additional recording would be slotted in between gigs and promo dates over the next 15 months, running through to February 2019.

Photography for the cover artwork of *Office Politics* took place in March 2019 and was shot by photographer Ben Meadows, who had previously been employed for photography on the DLM album *Sticky Wickets*. The artwork for *Office Politics* is an obvious doff-of-the-cap to the artwork inside the gatefold sleeve of 10cc's 1976 album *How Dare You!*. On the front cover, Hannon is engaged with a telephone call in the foreground, while other assorted employees seem to be partaking in a laid-back office party scenario all around him.

Office Politics was released on 7 June 2019 and garnered some positive reviews. *Classic Pop* reckoned that '*Office Politics* is already one of the year's most articulate records', adding: 'It boasts wit, wisdom and warmth'. *Music OMH* chipped in with, 'Hannon's mind-bendingly catchy couplets haunt the edges of this record', and *XS Noize* confirmed: 'The trademark eccentric, irreverent wit and reflective melodies are all present here' on a 'weird, fun and zesty record'. In the UK album chart, *Office Politics* shot in at number five on its release, but again, its chart run was brief, once the initial burst of sales from the hardcore DC fan base subsided.

'Queuejumper' (Hannon)

The first single release from the album is a song with a heavily percussive attack, powered by no less than three drummers; along with regular DC drummer Tim Weller, both Tosh Flood and Andrew Skeet are also whacking the skins here. Opening with various percussion instruments and some synthesiser noises that sound like a stray cat on heat, the track soon settles into an up-tempo beat, recalling the rhythm of the 1956 hit 'Giddy-Up-A-Ding-Dong' by Freddie Bell & The Bell Boys. Over the lively, jumping beat, Hannon's vocal melody follows a perky marimba-like line, most likely played by him on one of the many classic synthesisers employed on this recording.

What better way to start a concept album exploring aspects of the world of work than with a bright and breezy song about an upstart commuter who jumps the traffic queue, claiming to be 'smarter than you' and believing that 'Red lights don't apply to me'. The nagging verse melody is infectious and Hannon's rhythmic piano, underpinning the choruses, works well and, to my ears, brings to mind the rhythm of The Tremeloes' 1967 hit version of the Cat Stevens song 'Here Comes My Baby'. To top it off, a smart middle eight breaks up the action, adding a nice sense of balance to the song.

'Office Politics' (Hannon)

Veering between a mechanistic beat and a soul/funk feel, the title track describes a scenario that will be familiar to those of us who have worked in an office. Some notable characters appear in the lyrics, including the boss Sir Hillary, a chap called Knox (who will reappear later in the album), Zara Brewster (bringing forth the priceless line: 'Thus spake Zara Brewster'!) and a certain William, who, in fact, turns out to be none other than former international business traveller Billy Bird, last encountered on the *Absent Friends* album in 2004. He is also referred to again later in the album. The usual office shenanigans are all here, including taking a ride on the photocopier and posting the resultant dodgy photos on social media. Hannon raps the lyrics over a slow beat, accompanied by funky rhythm guitar work and staccato, James Brown-style brass. The guitar work really cooks up some funk towards the end of the track, and soulful wailing from the trio of Hazel Fernandes, Sonia Jones and Katie Kissoon on backing vocals adds to the soul feel of this track.

'Norman And Norma' (Hannon)

Andrew Skeet's piano intro leads into a classic example of Hannon's ability to dream up a perfect pop melody as he regales the tale of a working-class couple and their married life together. The story opens in Cromer, on the Norfolk coast, in April 1983, where Norman and Norma take their vows, subsequently honeymooning in Majorca. The chorus is joyous and catchy, built on a rhythm similar to The Ronettes' 1963 hit 'Be My Baby'. As their story unfolds, we learn that the couple had three lovely daughters, with the amusingly alliterative names 'Nadia, Norah and Neive'. Sadly, Norma loses her job after maternity leave and Norman's salary won't now stretch to holidaying in Majorca, cueing up the amusing Hannon rhyming couplet: 'So they went to Cromer' and 'got double pneumonia'. The verse melody has a slowly rising feel that builds to the irresistible sing-along choruses and the arrangement has some lovely touches. This is cushioned in a wash from a trio of different synthesisers, played by Hannon, as well as acoustic and 12-string guitars and some perfect touches from his electric guitar – check out the guitar figure that pulls away after the first line of the last couple of choruses.

The last verse rejoins the couple 20 years on, with the kids now having flown the coop. Despite 'salsa classes' and 'growing tomatoes', nothing is getting the couple off until, on a visit to the Essex seaside town of Clacton, they come across an enactment of the Norman invasion (that French connection again!). This 'gets their juices flowing', and very soon, they are dressing up in costume and 'fighting like it's 1066'. The choruses are buoyed by the female backing vocals of the Fernandes/Jones/Kissoon trio, adding harmonic depth. All in all, this was a worthy second single from the album that, in an earlier era, would surely have been a chart certainty.

'Absolutely Obsolete' (Hannon)

Looking at another aspect of the world of work – redundancy and obsolescence – is this fascinating mix of funk and electronics, and even, in the middle eight, a touch of music hall influence. In the verses, the lyrics explore the ever-encroaching role of machines and apps replacing the human element in the workforce. Of musical note is the two-note harmonic motif after the first and third lines of each verse, shifting momentarily out of the home key – an imaginative touch. The choruses groove on a funky rhythm guitar figure around one chord, played by Tosh Flood, giving them a somewhat monotone feel. This emphasises the mechanistic aspect of the subject matter, that of machines replacing humans for more and more tasks. The arrangement is given interest, however, by a casual French horn line that shadows the choruses. It's easy to spot the recognisable voice of studio guest Chris Difford from Squeeze on these choruses, singing along with Cathy Davey and Thomas Walsh.

The middle eight is a wonderful passage. It brings the human element back in, albeit with a hint of sadness, as the music briefly turns to a jaunty, music hall style, strongly evoking The Kinks' Ray Davies at his most whimsical. Here, the protagonist of the song yearns to turn the clock back to simpler times, 'when the world was black and white', instead of 'just shades of grey'. This section has a real end-of-the-pier feeling to it, enhanced by Hannon's mandolin, glockenspiel and Mellotron contributions. This brief sunny interlude is soon subsumed back into the mechanistic chorus, which is repeated to bring the song to a close.

'Infernal Machines' (Hannon)

After two gong crashes and a brass fanfare of some grandiosity, this track confounds expectations by kicking into a 1970s Glitter Band-style drum rhythm. The Glitter-related similarities don't end there either, as a perpetually repeating riff of utter simplicity drives the track forward in a mechanistic and relentless way, creating a decidedly menacing forward thrust. It sounds remarkably like the Mike Leander-masterminded guitar sound employed on those early 1970s Gary Glitter records he produced. It's so close that it could actually pass for a sample of said guitar sound, although Tosh Flood is credited with playing an Eastwood Baritone electric guitar, which is perhaps combined with one of the synthesisers played by Hannon to create this monstrous sound.

The lyrics slavishly follow the riff melody, such as it is, adding to the robotic feel of the music. It works a treat when combined with the lyrics, as they warn us against the ultimate cost of transferring too much power over to machines. Practically every line starts with the word 'machines' as we contemplate mechanisation-gone-mad, with machines that 'go ping', 'go pong' and think 'that they know right from wrong', as well as performing myriad other functions. Unfortunately, this includes machines that 'will make mistakes', Hannon's lyric wisely pointing out, 'that is the trouble with infernal machines'.

There is something hypnotically alluring in the unbending rhythmic repetitiveness of this track, and Hannon throws in a few experimental ideas over the top, including a playfully dissonant keyboard riff atop one of the verses – a knowing nod to the avant-garde, with its subtle key-clashes. There are various sound effects applied by bassist Simon Little and some backing vocal chants of the title from Thomas Walsh. The song closes by melding into the following track, with which it was paired on a 7" single, released in October 2019.

'You'll Never Work In This Town Again' (Hannon, Morales, Blanco, Leonard, Sunshine)

The credits for this Neil Hannon song take in the fact that it features samples from Percy Faith's recording of the Latin American composition 'Enlloro (Voodoo Moon)' from his 1952 album *Carnival Rhythms*. The result is a track with a genuine Latin vibe that sways along on a two-note bass line, while percussion and brass really cook up a hot salsa sauce, especially in the instrumental break. As well as playing Jumbo organ, Hannon adds some atmospheric harmonica work. His album credits also include 'Percy Faith cut-ups'.

Lyrically, the theme follows smoothly from 'Infernal Machines' and raises the ghost of Ned Ludd – whose name was appropriated by the 'Luddite' movement in the early 19th century. As Hannon's lyrics elucidate, Ludd was a harassed working man who destroyed an early version of mechanisation in a fit of pique – thus, a legend was born.

The dream of machines making life easier can lead to undesirable consequences, as Hannon expresses with the line: 'Well, here it is your life of ease' – an outcome that often results in loss of employment for redundant staff. This is encapsulated in the catchy chorus chant of the song title. To underline the fact that this is an ongoing situation, these days with computers, Hannon sings of 'that crazy algorithm' taking over all aspects of our lives, both work and leisure, as more and more of us become entranced and hypnotised by modern technology, fostering a concomitant neglect of our more practical skills.

'Psychological Evaluation' (Hannon)

Next up is a strange one: a duo performance by just Neil Hannon and bassist Simon Little. The music very much takes a back seat here, as Hannon is quizzed by a computer attempting to assess his psyche – leading to many amusing responses to the computer's questions. Apart from Little's bass line, Hannon provides all the instrumentation on this track, including Yamaha Portasound PSS-170, Mini-Nova, Mellotron, Prophet 5 synthesiser and drums. The questioning computer voice sounds heavily processed, making it difficult to clearly hear the questions, but Hannon's replies are the real rib-tickling moments here, the best trio of these being: *Q: 'Waste products?'* – A: 'Firm, if slightly irregular'; *Q: 'Emotions?'* – A: 'Hmmm'; *Q: 'Regrets?'* – A: 'I've had a few. Should have learned French' (the last of these, with its 'My Way' connotation, really tickled my funny bone the first time I heard it!). The two choruses find the computer voice analysing the results of its questioning as it goes along, deciding that it's *'Too soon to draw a conclusion regarding human evolution'*. The interrogation ends with the question: *'Music?'*. Hannon replies with a list of 23 of his favourite 1980s, mainly electro-pop acts. As the track fades, it eventually segues, rather suitably, into the next one, a celebratory inventory of classic synthesizers for sale, hopefully with a generous discount applied!

'The Synthesizer Service Centre Super Summer Sale' (Hannon, Skeet, Watson, Weller, Flood, Little)

With a backing track performed on 11 whirring, throbbing, wailing and oscillating synthesisers, set against a sequenced-synthesiser line and occasional intrusions by a Roland-808 drum machine, this is the first group composition to appear on a Divine Comedy album. Over the amusingly chaotic background, Hannon plays the role of synthesiser salesman, plugging his wares with tongue-twisting alliteration. As he goes into his sales pitch rap, fans of 1980s synthesisers will find many of their old favourites mentioned here, as well as more recent products. My particular fancy back in the 1980s was the Godwin string synthesiser (not mentioned here), which, along with the Fairlight sampler (which is mentioned here), I employed extensively when recording my own 1989 album *Earth Magic*.

Definitely funnier the first time you hear it, this tongue-twisting ode to everything synthesised still works well as a light-hearted interlude, adding to the album's balance of light and shade.

'The Life And Soul Of The Party' (Hannon)

Opening with crowd noises to let us know that it's time for the office party, we find ourselves firmly in the disco zone via this upbeat parody, which introduces us to that one-at-every-party phenomenon: the embarrassingly inebriated buffoon, competing to be the centre of attention. There's no doubt about it; from the cover artwork down, this album owes a debt to 10cc. This track, in particular, while reminding me of the middle section of 'The Anonymous Alcoholic' from 10cc's 1978 album *Bloody Tourists*, also employs the device of juxtaposing high and low voices to give definition to the song's characters. This is a device with a venerable history, from The Ink Spots in the 1930s, The Coasters in the 1950s, The Temptations in the 1960s/1970s and a classic hallmark of 10cc in the 1970s.

Hannon's lyrics depict the ever-worsening drunken state of the song's protagonist, while the deep-voiced chorus chants of the title are performed by most of the band, plus engineer Jake Jackson. The female vocal trio throw in some soulful response vocals during the verses and the whole thing grooves along in a highly danceable fashion. By the close of the song, it's hard not to feel sorry for the drunken sot, who by now, is talking to his beer and mumbling to himself because 'I'm all alone in here'.

'A Feather In Your Cap' (Hannon)

This track is a solo performance by Neil Hannon on a variety of keyboards, including Prophet 5, Mini-Nova, Jumbo, SV-1 and Solina (also marketed as the ARP), as well as vocals. It has a lighter-than-air feel and nods to a Philly-soul influence. Using one of the keyboards to generate a gentle electric piano sound, the arrangement starts sparsely on the verses before building up via string samples for the plaintive second section of the song.

Hannon's lyrics, on the subject of a brief relationship that he hoped would be more than just 'a notch upon your bedpost', evince a resigned sadness. Whether he is singing from a personal perspective or playing a part in a character-driven song is uncertain, but the performance does sound as if it's coming from the heart. It's a sweet and sad little song.

'I'm A Stranger Here' (Hannon)

The sound of lone footsteps moving across the stereo picture opens this haunting song. The style here very much evokes the atmosphere of 1930s Berlin cabaret, with a strong European flavour. The arrangement is understated for the most part and creeps along in a state of shadowy melancholia. It's one of those songs liable to reverberate deeply with many listeners of a certain vintage, dealing as it does with the sense of alienation often experienced as one grows older and struggles to adapt to a world where all the old certainties have departed. The choruses are bolstered by Hannon's mandolin, enhancing the European vibe and adding to the poignancy, expressing a sense of loss and a feeling of isolation.

The middle eight is a classic Hannon construction, as the Mellotron momentarily breaks the slowly creeping feel of the verses with a sudden surge of sound (and possibly hope), but quickly reverts back to a haunted feel, as Hannon sings: 'If you ask where I come from, I'll say 'the past' and wander on'. There follows a spooky return of the Germanic-sounding verse melody played on what sounds like a bassoon and accompanied by drunken-sounding, sliding string glissandos – an extraordinary passage that exacerbates the eerie ambience of its melody. One more mandolin-heavy chorus leads us to an ending chord that sounds like a musical question mark. If you listen very carefully after this chord, you will hear the verse melody resume, but played extremely quietly, sounding as if it's emanating from behind some locked door, way down a long corridor – it's a chilling effect. The organ then faintly starts to play the 1929 Milton Ager/Jack Yellen song 'Happy Days Are Here Again', before running out of steam and dying away, making for a perfect, contrasting juxtaposition with the next track.

'Dark Days Are Here Again' (Hannon)

Descending like a dark cloud of foreboding, massed bass voices ominously chant the song title, underpinned by a slow keyboard arpeggio, which moves in crotchets to and fro across the sound picture. As the first doom-laden verse crashes in, the sound is dark, massive and heavy, akin to the earthshaking, slow stomp of a hacked-off tyrannosaur after a bad night's sleep.

Hannon's lyrics ponder the unthinkable, as he mourns losing the good times that came and went, leaving us stranded in 'the winter of our discontent'. Perhaps influenced by the parlous state of the US presidency around the time this album was recorded, as well as the ever-worsening climate emergency, the lyrics rue the 'day we thought would never come' when 'a veil was drawn across the sun'. Evincing a sense of doom, the words are matched by the lugubrious music.

In a brilliant demonstration of the use of dynamics, all becomes still and quiet for a central instrumental interlude. This passage is musically identical to the verse but performed in a very different way. Andrew Skeet's piano trips lightly over the treble keys, demonstrating that the verse melody is actually a beautiful but sad air, with more than a hint of classicism about it. Ian Watson's accordion accentuates the European feel of Hannon's sorrowful tune and this lovely interlude leads back into a grosser version of the same music. As the second verse crunches in, it seems even heavier on the beat than the first verse. Each half-bar thud is akin to a pile-driver hitting the ground, as Tosh Flood bends his strings across the guitar fretboard, increasing a building tension that finds no release. Skeet's portentous, chromatic run of semiquavers on the deepest notes of the piano emphasises some of the chord changes in the verse – they are dramatic and crushingly powerful.

The song moves to a close with the bass voices repeating the intro section, while Omnichord, Mellotron and a bass drone rack up more intensity, until it all suddenly cuts to the female backing singers, chirping anachronistically with soulful, upbeat voices, singing: 'Dark days are here again'.

'Philip And Steve's Furniture Removal Company' (Hannon)
As explained by Hannon before the track proper kicks in, this piece evolved from an idea for a sitcom, based on the early lives of minimalist composers Philip Glass and Steve Reich in New York, back in the 1960s. Hannon amusingly adds that it will feature 'Many hilarious gags about the repetitive nature of the work'.

He then kicks off proceedings acapella-style, initiating a repeating one-bar chant of the song title in 9/4 time, which is subsequently supported by rapid handclaps. In line with minimalist procedure, this melodic fragment is repeated, but then shifted slightly out of alignment as it proceeds, so that the duplicated, overlapping vocals create new harmonic possibilities as the piece progresses. It's amazing how complex something can become from a simple, repeated fragment. Eventually, a marimba sample, played by Andrew Skeet, takes over the melodic riff and the track gradually builds as different piano and synthesised string chords are placed beneath the repeating line, leading to new harmonic variations.

There is a rap by Hannon later in the track, his phrases treated the same way as the initial material: being moved out of alignment and overlapped. This rap expands on the plot of the purported sitcom and is highly amusing. It advertises the minimalist duo's furniture removal company, who, with 'minimal disruption to your routine', can rescue your home from the atonal 'Boulez-loving lout' who previously scuffed all your furniture. Not only will they do this for you, but they'll do it 'again and again and again'. If you can tolerate a good deal of repetition, this track is really good fun and gets us back on a humorous tack after the heaviness of the previous song. By the close of the song, there is a massed choir of voices singing the title riff, making it sound like some demented, off-kilter opera. Now, with synthesised backing playing the melodic riff under the choral voices, it is suddenly brought to a close by Hannon's vocals singing one last repetition. In its own quirky way, this is something of a minimalist mini-masterpiece.

"Opportunity' Knox' (Hannon)
Displaying some conceptual continuity, we are re-introduced to a certain Mr Knox, who appeared earlier on the album's title track. However, we learn a good deal more about his personality here. The track starts with a knock upon a door and an invitation to enter, and it seems we are back at the premises of the company we visited on the album's title track, as Mr Knox steps into the office of Ms Monroe (possibly the firm's Human Resources Manager?). Knox attempts to persuade her to consider him for the position

now vacant, following the recent mysterious disappearance of Billy Bird. The dubious Mr Knox further besmirches Bird's reputation with the intimation that he was 'taking liberties with the company accounts'.

The musical soundtrack to this saga takes the rhythmic form of a slowed-down Russian Cossack dance, with Andrew Skeet's piano chords as a foundation and Ian Watson's accordion providing an authentic Russian folk flavour. On the sing-along choruses, the majority of the band chip in on the 'opportunities' and 'la-la-la' chants, while Tosh Flood provides some low-voiced backing vocals of the song title.

By the third verse, we start to suspect that Billy Bird's disappearance involved more than financial skulduggery, as uniformed police turn up at the company headquarters to 'have a word' with Mr Knox 'concerning William Bird'. The characterisations in this verse are excellent and rather funny, as Knox admits to having a drink with Bird, protesting, 'this isn't blood it's ink'. As the amusement quotient racks up, there are several great lines, 'so, I've got muddy shoes, what's that to do with you?', and the final giveaway to Bird's fate, as Knox affirms: 'to own a shovel isn't odd'. As the incorrigible Mr Knox is collared by the long arm of the law and led away, his last words to Ms Monroe are: 'Just tell me if I got the job'. This galvanising mini-play closes with another round of its catchy chorus, but this time, it speeds up as it goes, just like an authentic Russian Cossack dance, finally coming to a dead-stop ending.

'After The Lord Mayor's Show' (Hannon)

Taking the form of a slow march, this piano-led ballad plays on the well-known saying: 'After the Lord Mayor's show, comes the donkey cart'. The arrangement is kept fairly simple, with Andrew Skeet's piano chords and some fine military snare drumming by Tim Weller cushioned by Neil Hannon's Mellotron and decorated by some tasteful playing from the brass section. The song is gently climactic, with a slow build-up. Hannon's vocals are superbly augmented by the response vocals of the female backing trio of Fernandes, Jones and Kissoon, who have made a distinctive contribution to a large part of this album.

It's a song that reflects on the fact that 'when the glory boys depart', in many ways, 'that's when the real work starts'. It may be a reflection on how Hannon views The Divine Comedy in the scheme of things; as a slowly building, substantial body of work over a longer time frame compared to the more ephemeral pop sensations that come and go with such regularity.

'When The Working Day Is Done' (Hannon)

A factory whistle introduces the second march in a row – this time, though, a more brisk one. This track is a development of an earlier musical idea, first attempted on the 2010 download release 'Beside The Railway Tracks' – a bonus track with the iTunes version of *Bang Goes The Knighthood*. On the earlier version, the lyrics concerned a misfit who lived adjacent to a railway track. It had a heavily processed vocal, which, compared with this revision, sounded somewhat underdeveloped. Neil Hannon sticks to guitars and vocals here, leaving piano duties to Andrew Skeet and Mellotron to Ian Watson. It's another track with a fabulous build-up and a chord sequence that gives a feeling of perpetual ascent as the arrangement becomes more and more full, eventually bringing in the entire orchestra over a constant forward march. It is somehow both a celebration of and a lament for the workers of the world. On an album that began with a song about commuting to work, this song completes the cycle by describing the journey home from the day's labours. There is some nice shading from major to minor keys throughout, with many moving lyrical touches en route, observed with Hannon's usual cinematic eye and attention to detail that makes you feel as if you are there, packed in the train on the homeward commute. It's a track that gives a feeling of completeness to the 'working day' concept explored on *Office Politics* and makes a perfect ending to this adventurous and wide-ranging album.

Charmed Life – Super Extra Bonus Album (2022)

Personnel:
Neil Hannon: vocals, guitars, keyboards
Andrew Skeet: piano, backing vocals
Tosh Flood: guitar, keyboards, backing vocals
Ian Watson: accordion, piano, backing vocals
Simon Little: bass, backing vocals
Tim Weller: drums, percussion
Margaret Shanley: vocals ('Who Do You Think You Are')
Thomas Walsh: backing vocals ('I'll Take What I Can Get')
Jake Jackson: backing vocals ('I'll Take What I Can Get', 'The Adventurous Type')
Cathy Davey: backing vocals ('Te Amo Espana')
Chris Worsey, Ian Burdge, Steve Morris, Lucy Wilkins, Nicky Sweeney, Marianne Haynes, Simon Baggs, Perry Montague-Mason, Peter Hanson, Reiad Chibah, Emma Owens, Richard Pryce, Warren Zielinski, Richard George, Bruce White: strings
Strings arranged and conducted by Andrew Skeet; additional string arrangements by Neil Hannon; strings contracted by Lucy Whalley
London Accordion Orchestra: orchestrated and conducted by Ian Watson ('I'll Take What I Can Get', 'The Adventurous Type')
Recorded at Snap Studios, London; Sonic and Herbert Place, Dublin; AIR (London) Studios; AIR Edel Studios, London between 2020 and 2021
Engineers: Ber Quinn, Guy Massey, Jake Jackson and Nick Taylor
Mixed by Guy Massey
Mastered by Frank Arkwright at Abbey Road Studios, London
Producer: Neil Hannon
Record label: Divine Comedy Records
Released: 4 February 2022
Highest UK chart position: 5

Following the release of *Office Politics*, The Divine Comedy began rehearsing in September 2019 in preparation for a tour to promote the new album. This tour kicked off in Dublin on 6 October, moving on to Belfast and Cork, before hitting the UK mainland. For the London gig at Hammersmith Apollo, the band played 11 songs from the new album and a generous selection of old favourites, stretching back to the early 1990s. They opened the set with one of Neil Hannon's earliest songs 'Europop', and closed the show, after five encores, with the much-adored DC classic 'Tonight We Fly'. After the UK dates came trips through Holland, Germany, Belgium, France, Spain and Portugal. No one could accuse Neil Hannon of slowing down in his 49th year!

2020 marked the 30th anniversary of The Divine Comedy and this was commemorated with the release of the luxurious 24-disc box set *Venus, Cupid, Folly And Time*, replete with 2-CD editions of all the studio albums, along with various bonus CDs. These extras included *Juveneilia*: a compilation of pre-Divine Comedy recordings, some of which were touched upon in my earlier 'Introduction' chapter. Many of the extra tracks included with each album had been previously released on singles and EPs, the more interesting of these I have discussed in the relevant chapters. Any prospective purchaser of this box set will need deep pockets, as it was a limited edition, originally retailing at around £125, but has since been made unavailable, so you would be very lucky to obtain one for under £300 at the time of writing!

In February 2022, there was a nice surprise for DC fans in the shape of the 3-CD set *Charmed Life – The Best Of The Divine Comedy*. Ostensibly a 'Best Of' compilation, it became an essential purchase for DC fans, as it had a whole CD of new material included in the shape of the *Super Extra Bonus Album*. This consisted of a batch of songs mostly written by Neil Hannon during the 2020 COVID-19 lockdown and this fact is reflected in some of the lyrics.

Charmed Life briefly returned The Divine Comedy to the upper reaches of the UK album chart, peaking at number five. It represented a fine selection of DC classics from Hannon's ongoing 32-year recording career, but for hardcore DC fans, it was the *Super Extra Bonus Album* that was the package's most essential element.

'I'll Take What I Can Get' (Hannon)

Opening with a series of guitar arpeggios akin to aural question marks, we're soon into a cyclic, circular chord sequence, powered by chunky electric guitars. This sequence continually resolves itself back to its starting point. This suits the lyrics admirably, as Neil Hannon lists all the things he intends to do 'one day' with an opposing list of what he'll do 'till then'. As ever with Hannon, this leads to many amusing 'one day' resolutions, including 'I'll be frightfully arty' (mission accomplished, I would say!), 'I'll write my symphony' (this one wouldn't surprise me) and, in a humorous nod to the famous James Joyce novel, 'I'll finish Ulysses'. The 'till then' list will be familiar to those of us who procrastinate about embarking on our own personal ambitions, and instead end up putting off decisions, watching TV or struggling to get out of bed. In the latter part of the song's arrangement, Ian Watson conducts the London Accordion Orchestra, as they provide a cascading waterfall of chromatic up-and-down accordion runs that help propel the song to its climax, where it suddenly falls back to, and closes with, the quizzical guitar arpeggios that opened it.

'Don't Make Me Go Outside' (Hannon)

Next up is an anthem for agoraphobics everywhere, a condition that a lot more people ended up struggling with after the 2020 COVID-19 lockdown. Quite a few of the songs on this album were obviously influenced by the lockdown experiences we all went through in this period, resulting in what is very much Hannon's 'lockdown album', with direct references on three of the ten tracks featured.

This song has a delicate, light-as-a-feather feel based around a strummed ukulele. It is given its distinctive character by a clever arrangement for Chris Worsey's cello and Bruce White's viola, the two string lines twisting playfully around each other like a brace of amorous butterflies in flight. With its economical arrangement, the song displays a nice sense of uncluttered space, in sympathy with its pleading lyric. Hannon sings a lovely, simple melody that, when combined with the lyrics and airy arrangement, is a pure delight to listen to.

'Who Do You Think You Are' (Hannon)

This dance track is a temporal, don't-end-up-like-us message in a bottle to our remote ancestors, awaiting delivery via a convenient wormhole time-warp, hopefully with a 'universal translator' thrown in. The opening vocal chorus is heavily processed via the use of autotune, employing one of its more extreme settings – a sound that would certainly startle any denizen of the palaeolithic era, that's for sure!

The verses start with a catchy rap of 'Hey mister proto-human *homo habilis*' and issue a warning to ignore 'that big black obelisk' (a wry reference to Arthur C. Clarke's sci-fi novel *2001: A Space Odyssey*, or more specifically, Stanley Kubrick's 1968 film adaption of the novel). The up-tempo dance beat is contagious and is buoyed by some hummable synthesiser lines. There is a dynamic, stop-time break, where Hannon dispenses further strong advice to our unwitting antecedents to 'Stay in your rift valley, even if it's a blind alley', followed by a further admonition to 'Put down that crudely fashioned tool, and don't be a fool'.

The chorus returns once more to ram home the message that if these distant proto-humans realised they were likely to evolve into the current mess that passes for human endeavour, they very well might do, as Hannon suggests, to 'climb back up your family tree'. There you go – you can't say they haven't been warned – now, where's that wormhole?

'The Adventurous Type' (Hannon)

One of the highlights of the album, this memorably mad track opens with honky-tonk, barroom piano and a good-time vibe, playing a tune that will later provide the sing-along choruses. Featuring a piano duet between Ian Watson and Andrew Skeet, it soon rolls from the barroom opening into an insanely brisk march, propelled by Tim Weller's snare drum. The pianos crash and bash around and the London Accordion Orchestra fills out the sound picture with aplomb. Once this soundtrack is combined with Hannon's frantic vocals, it brings to mind the feeling of watching an old Mack Sennett slapstick comedy, back in the era of silent movies, to a manic musical accompaniment.

Hannon excels here, both in storytelling and comedic terms, as the protagonist of the song longs to be the adventurous type and embarks on a haphazard day where caution is thrown to the wind. In an attempt to 'do something rash, and see where it goes', he sticks out his thumb and gets picked up by an 'interesting group of guys' who turn out to be tattooed, knife-wielding skinheads! After drinking at a bar with his new pals, he ducks out into an alley, but 'into the midst of a fascist rally'. These reprobates proceed to goose-step through the bar (the discordant accordion riff here amusingly punctuates the action), while his former cronies are now singing 'death to all adventurous types'. To make the situation even more chaotic, the police raid the bar, and in the ensuing melee of tear gas and truncheons, he is 'hit by a bottle and slumps to the floor'. The barroom choruses of 'I want to know what it's like' follow the action-packed verses with a good-time cheer, as the song veers crazily between the sing-along choruses and Keystone Cops-style action in the verses.

The third verse is an absolute killer, with a magnificent punch line. It's sung in a becalmed mode to a gentle piano accompaniment and sees our protagonist wake up from his bottle-induced daze to find his watch, wallet and 'most of his hair' missing. He appears to be on a boat, pitching and yawing on the sea, with no land in sight. This leads us to the priceless punch line: 'Oh my God. What a brilliant night'. The comic timing in Hannon's delivery of this line had me rolling with mirth the first time I heard it.

The song then plays out, repeating its rolling chorus, sounding like an East End knees-up, as the barroom pianos roll and the accordions swing and pump along, including some punctuating triplets towards the end. The whole thing then seems to vanish, as if through a stage trapdoor, ending a rip-roaringly hilarious performance.

'When When When' (Hannon)

This opens with a touching prelude, underpinned by sparse piano chords, returning us to the subject of the COVID-19 lockdown as Neil Hannon ponders on the imposed isolation it fostered. It finds him working on jigsaws retrieved from his attic (having now 'finished the Sistine Chapel', he is just 'starting on Big Ben').

Then, as Tim Weller's drums take up a measured 12/8 rhythm, Richard Pryce provides string bass accompaniment, along with Hannon's piano marking time, and we're firmly into MOR territory – veering close to cliché, but purposely so. The old-time ambience of this ballad takes this particular listener right back to a childhood in the East End of London in the 1960s. Settled in bed on sultry hot weekend evenings, my ears were regaled by the sound of the then-middle-aged drinkers crooning old standards and pub songs while gathered around a piano and drums duo, who were bashing away in the pub on the corner of our street – it's a sound that used to drift me off to sleep!

By this juncture, it becomes clear that, with a few exceptions, this is very much Neil Hannon's easy-listening album, as MOR influences abound in most of the songs. Like everything he turns his hand to, though, he is as much at home with this genre of music as he is with his more experimental and exploratory material.

It's a familiar-sounding sequence, with a rising verse melody, and could almost be related to Chas & Dave's 1982 hit single 'Ain't No Pleasing You', which was composed in a similar vein and employed a virtually identical rhythm, albeit at a slightly faster tempo. In the lyrics, Hannon pines for the day he can be reunited with his loved one and it certainly brings back those dark days of lockdown we all went through in 2020. The track is nicely orchestrated and, like the rest of this album, is extremely pleasant to listen to, especially when in the mood for something lighter to enjoy.

'Home For The Holidays' (Hannon)

Stop Press: 'The Divine Comedy record Christmas song' shock! It's not a genre I'm personally a fan of as a rule, but as usual, Hannon's sense of quality control shines through, giving this one something special. A highly appealing melody lends this performance its particular gleam and it helps that the song does not mention the word 'Christmas' every ten seconds (in fact, it only mentions that word once).

Hannon's piano underpins the arrangement and there are various sparkly sound effects added like aural frosting, as the song mentions various Yuletide things. There's also a nice use of repeat echoes on the backing vocals, especially the 'ho, ho, ho's thrown in after certain lines. It's a song that evokes driving through the snow, with the line, 'playing Perry Como, as we go', perhaps accounting for the easy listening bias on display on much of this album. It's a likeable song and even manages a touch of poignancy, along with the festive cheer, especially with the line, 'But there's an empty chair, say a prayer', nodding to the inevitable loss of a loved one, as the passage of time rushes ever onward.

'Te Amo Espana' (Hannon)

Yet another lockdown song – and this time, it's pining for a time when a Spanish holiday will be back on the cards again. Hannon whips out his Spanish guitar to provide some tasty flamenco licks and the music is full of light-hearted Iberian charm.

There are many amusing couplets to savour here and Hannon's cod-Spanish is a constant source of delight. As he points out in the lyrics: 'Enrique y Julio Iglesias, taught me all these Spanish phrases'. Some trumpet fanfares decorate this arrangement, although, oddly, no trumpet player is mentioned in the album credits. This song, in effusive praise of all things Spanish, is jolly good fun, and in the final verse, Hannon avers. 'One day when the lockdown is over, we'll get on the ferry at Dover'. This is followed by a drive down to the border to once again wallow in the sun, sea, sand and culture of that sunny destination.

'Perfect Lovesong 2021' (Hannon)

This is pretty much a straight remake of a song first featured on the album *Regeneration*. There are minor differences, but it's hard to see why it was re-recorded for this album (unless Hannon just fancied having another go at it). On balance, the original 2001 version has a touch more magic to it than this remake. It's still a great song, though.

'Simple Pleasures' (Hannon)

Here's a song about the little things in life that really matter – simple pleasures. Everyone has their own personal list of the small things that make life worthwhile, and in this song, Neil Hannon shares some of those special moments with his listeners. Set to a mid-pace tempo and powered by simple guitar riffs, this little beauty grooves along nicely. As well as Simon Little's electric bass, this also features Richard Pryce on string bass. Furthermore, a pair of cellos, played by Chris Worsey and Ian Burdge, enhance the addictive rhythm of this song, tidily arranged by Andrew Skeet. The vocal melody is simple but compelling and an unidentified band member whistles along with it at one point – it's that kind of tune.

'Those Pesky Kids' (Hannon)

Musically, the triple time arrangement of this song sounds like a definite nod to Joe Cocker & The Grease Band's 1969 hit single version of the Lennon/McCartney song 'With A Little Help From My Friends'. The slow tempo, Hannon's organ chords and Tosh Flood's keening lead guitar lines towards the end magnify the comparison to the Cocker hit.

Lyrically, it sees a resurgence of Hannon's ongoing interest in all things green. It seems to have been influenced by the inspiring sight of the many very young but knowledgeable environmental protesters who were often in the news around the time this album was recorded. Sadly, much of the momentum gained in efforts to persuade governments to put more resources towards tackling the climate emergency seems to have been reversed in the last couple of years, as more immediately pressing issues, caused by unnecessary conflict and human suffering, took centre stage. This song is performed from the point of view of the archetypal, rich, corporate fat cat along the lines of: 'If it weren't for those pesky kids, we'd have got away with it'. The song is broken up by a bridge in which the unnamed tycoon chants: 'Stealing their future was meant to be easy'. My sympathies are with the kids on this one!

'Piste 11' (Hannon)

This short, quirky experiment is a hidden track, closing the album. Over a circulating piano motif, sounding like currents of air, Hannon chants, 'I'm a little butterfly', while a young child's voice, recorded at a low level in the background, reflects his vocals with a monologue. The music dances and floats as if it's at the whim of a light breeze.

It is perhaps referential to the 'butterfly effect' and chaos theory previously conjured 24 years earlier on the track 'The Certainty Of Chance' from *Fin De Siecle*. This possibly links it to Hannon's environmental concerns; maybe the piste of the title is now melting due to global warming. This would mark the track as a further, if rather oblique, comment on how the very small (the butterfly) can eventually affect the very large (the environment), and, by inference, how more gross human actions can significantly affect the biosphere. Whatever the authorial intention is, it certainly provides a suitably surreal conclusion to the *Super Extra Bonus Album*.

Additional Material

'The Best Mistakes' (Hannon)

This excellent pop song slots in admirably among the hits and vintage album tracks of the 'Best Of' compilation selection and certainly holds its own in such an esteemed company. It sees Hannon reflecting on his wide-ranging career and coming to the conclusion that, although he has made mistakes, he wouldn't change a thing, as 'They were the best mistakes I've ever made'. It's a cannily constructed tune with an almost pop/soul feel, especially the elating choruses, bolstered by handclaps – it would've made a perfect single. The piano-led performance is well-orchestrated, and although Hannon admits that these days 'I kind of like remembering' the era of hits and pop stardom, he comes to the conclusion that, given the choice between then and now, 'I'd choose now'. It's the sound of a man who is happy in his skin.

Afterword

A joker, a genius or simply one of the most talented all-round musicians of his era, Neil Hannon seems to have all the bases covered. Hopefully, there'll be a lot more to come from this 'Renaissance Man' of pop in the near future. A new Hannon orchestral work – *As The Sun Brightens, The Shadows Deepen* – saw its world premiere at Ulster Hall, Belfast on 5 May 2023, as part of a concert programme that also featured another Hannon work: *To Our Fathers In Distress*, along with Khachaturian's *Adagio For Spartacus And Phrygia* and Vaughan Williams' *Norfolk Rhapsody No.1.* Also during 2023, The Divine Comedy performed a brace of summer festival dates at The Victorious Festival in Portsmouth on 26 August, and The Towersey Festival in Buckinghamshire on 27 August. On top of this, the dream team of Neil Hannon and Joby Talbot reunited in 2023 to provide the soundtrack for director Paul King's *Wonka* movie, a prequel to the classic 1971 film *Willy Wonka And The Chocolate Factory*. The new *Wonka* movie proved to be a smash number-one box office hit, while the Hannon/Talbot soundtrack received glowing reviews. Let's hope another new DC album will follow shortly. Meanwhile, for me and many other DC fans, listening to the already recorded output of The Divine Comedy is still – to quote an earlier lyric from the main man himself – 'Always a pleasure and never a chore'.

On Track Series

Allman Brothers Band – Andrew Wild 978-1-78952-252-5
Tori Amos – Lisa Torem 978-1-78952-142-9
Aphex Twin – Beau Waddell 978-1-78952-267-9
Asia – Peter Braidis 978-1-78952-099-6
Badfinger – Robert Day-Webb 978-1-878952-176-4
Barclay James Harvest – Keith And Monica Domone 978-1-78952-067-5
Beck – Arthur Lizie 978-1-78952-258-7
The Beatles – Andrew Wild 978-1-78952-009-5
The Beatles Solo 1969-1980 – Andrew Wild 978-1-78952-030-9
Blue Oyster Cult – Jacob Holm-Lupo 978-1-78952-007-1
Blur – Matt Bishop 978-178952-164-1
Marc Bolan And T.rex – Peter Gallagher 978-1-78952-124-5
Kate Bush – Bill Thomas 978-1-78952-097-2
Camel – Hamish Kuzminski 978-1-78952-040-8
Captain Beefheart – Opher Goodwin 978-1-78952-235-8
Caravan – Andy Boot 978-1-78952-127-6
Cardiacs – Eric Benac 978-1-78952-131-3
Nick Cave And The Bad Seeds – Dominic Sanderson 978-1-78952-240-2
Eric Clapton Solo – Andrew Wild 978-1-78952-141-2
The Clash – Nick Assirati 978-1-78952-077-4
Elvis Costello And The Attractions – Georg Purvis 978-1-78952-129-0
Crosby, Stills & Nash – Andrew Wild 978-1-78952-039-2
Creedence Clearwater Revival – Tony Thompson 978-178952-237-2
The Damned – Morgan Brown 978-1-78952-136-8
Deep Purple And Rainbow 1968-79 – Steve Pilkington 978-1-78952-002-6
Dire Straits – Andrew Wild 978-1-78952-044-6
The Doors – Tony Thompson 978-1-78952-137-5
Dream Theater – Jordan Blum 978-1-78952-050-7
Eagles – John Van Der Kiste 978-1-78952-260-0
Earth, Wind And Fire – Bud Wilkins 978-1-78952-272-3
Electric Light Orchestra – Barry Delve 978-1-78952-152-8
Emerson Lake And Palmer – Mike Goode 978-1-78952-000-2
Fairport Convention – Kevan Furbank 978-1-78952-051-4
Peter Gabriel – Graeme Scarfe 978-1-78952-138-2
Genesis – Stuart Macfarlane 978-1-78952-005-7
Gentle Giant – Gary Steel 978-1-78952-058-3
Gong – Kevan Furbank 978-1-78952-082-8
Green Day – William E. Spevack 978-1-78952-261-7
Hall And Oates – Ian Abrahams 978-1-78952-167-2
Hawkwind – Duncan Harris 978-1-78952-052-1
Peter Hammill – Richard Rees Jones 978-1-78952-163-4
Roy Harper – Opher Goodwin 978-1-78952-130-6

Jimi Hendrix – Emma Stott 978-1-78952-175-7
The Hollies – Andrew Darlington 978-1-78952-159-7
Horslips – Richard James 978-1-78952-263-1
The Human League And The Sheffield Scene –
Andrew Darlington 978-1-78952-186-3
The Incredible String Band – Tim Moon 978-1-78952-107-8
Iron Maiden – Steve Pilkington 978-1-78952-061-3
Joe Jackson – Richard James 978-1-78952-189-4
Jefferson Airplane – Richard Butterworth 978-1-78952-143-6
Jethro Tull – Jordan Blum 978-1-78952-016-3
Elton John In The 1970s – Peter Kearns 978-1-78952-034-7
Billy Joel – Lisa Torem 978-1-78952-183-2
Judas Priest – John Tucker 978-1-78952-018-7
Kansas – Kevin Cummings 978-1-78952-057-6
The Kinks – Martin Hutchinson 978-1-78952-172-6
Korn – Matt Karpe 978-1-78952-153-5
Led Zeppelin – Steve Pilkington 978-1-78952-151-1
Level 42 – Matt Philips 978-1-78952-102-3
Little Feat – Georg Purvis - 978-1-78952-168-9
Aimee Mann – Jez Rowden 978-1-78952-036-1
Joni Mitchell – Peter Kearns 978-1-78952-081-1
The Moody Blues – Geoffrey Feakes 978-1-78952-042-2
Motorhead – Duncan Harris 978-1-78952-173-3
Nektar – Scott Meze – 978-1-78952-257-0
New Order – Dennis Remmer – 978-1-78952-249-5
Nightwish – Simon Mcmurdo – 978-1-78952-270-9
Laura Nyro – Philip Ward 978-1-78952-182-5
Mike Oldfield – Ryan Yard 978-1-78952-060-6
Opeth – Jordan Blum 978-1-78-952-166-5
Pearl Jam – Ben L. Connor 978-1-78952-188-7
Tom Petty – Richard James 978-1-78952-128-3
Pink Floyd – Richard Butterworth 978-1-78952-242-6
The Police – Pete Braidis 978-1-78952-158-0
Porcupine Tree – Nick Holmes 978-1-78952-144-3
Queen – Andrew Wild 978-1-78952-003-3
Radiohead – William Allen 978-1-78952-149-8
Rancid – Paul Matts 989-1-78952-187-0
Renaissance – David Detmer 978-1-78952-062-0
Reo Speedwagon – Jim Romag 978-1-78952-262-4
The Rolling Stones 1963-80 – Steve Pilkington 978-1-78952-017-0
The Smiths And Morrissey – Tommy Gunnarsson 978-1-78952-140-5
Spirit – Rev. Keith A. Gordon – 978-1-78952- 248-8
Stackridge – Alan Draper 978-1-78952-232-7

Status Quo The Frantic Four Years – Richard James 978-1-78952-160-3
Steely Dan – Jez Rowden 978-1-78952-043-9
Steve Hackett – Geoffrey Feakes 978-1-78952-098-9
Tears For Fears – Paul Clark - 978-178952-238-9
Thin Lizzy – Graeme Stroud 978-1-78952-064-4
Tool – Matt Karpe 978-1-78952-234-1
Toto – Jacob Holm-Lupo 978-1-78952-019-4
U2 – Eoghan Lyng 978-1-78952-078-1
Ufo – Richard James 978-1-78952-073-6
Van Der Graaf Generator – Dan Coffey 978-1-78952-031-6
Van Halen – Morgan Brown – 9781-78952-256-3
The Who – Geoffrey Feakes 978-1-78952-076-7
Roy Wood And The Move – James R Turner 978-1-78952-008-8
Yes – Stephen Lambe 978-1-78952-001-9
Frank Zappa 1966 To 1979 – Eric Benac 978-1-78952-033-0
Warren Zevon – Peter Gallagher 978-1-78952-170-2
10cc – Peter Kearns 978-1-78952-054-5

Decades Series

The Bee Gees In The 1960s – Andrew Mon Hughes Et Al 978-1-78952-148-1
The Bee Gees In The 1970s – Andrew Mon Hughes Et Al 978-1-78952-179-5
Black Sabbath In The 1970s – Chris Sutton 978-1-78952-171-9
Britpop – Peter Richard Adams And Matt Pooler 978-1-78952-169-6
Phil Collins In The 1980s – Andrew Wild 978-1-78952-185-6
Alice Cooper In The 1970s – Chris Sutton 978-1-78952-104-7
Alice Cooper In The 1980s – Chris Sutton 978-1-78952-259-4
Curved Air In The 1970s – Laura Shenton 978-1-78952-069-9
Donovan In The 1960s – Jeff Fitzgerald 978-1-78952-233-4
Bob Dylan In The 1980s – Don Klees 978-1-78952-157-3
Brian Eno In The 1970s – Gary Parsons 978-1-78952-239-6
Faith No More In The 1990s – Matt Karpe 978-1-78952-250-1
Fleetwood Mac In The 1970s – Andrew Wild 978-1-78952-105-4
Fleetwood Mac In The 1980s – Don Klees 978-178952-254-9
Focus In The 1970s – Stephen Lambe 978-1-78952-079-8
Free And Bad Company In The 1970s – John Van Der Kiste 978-1-78952-178-8
Genesis In The 1970s – Bill Thomas 978178952-146-7
George Harrison In The 1970s – Eoghan Lyng 978-1-78952-174-0
Kiss In The 1970s – Peter Gallagher 978-1-78952-246-4
Manfred Mann's Earth Band In The 1970s – John Van Der Kiste 978178952-243-3
Marillion In The 1980s – Nathaniel Webb 978-1-78952-065-1
Van Morrison In The 1970s – Peter Childs - 978-1-78952-241-9
Mott The Hoople And Ian Hunter In The 1970s –

John Van Der Kiste 978-1-78-952-162-7
Pink Floyd In The 1970s – Georg Purvis 978-1-78952-072-9
Suzi Quatro In The 1970s – Darren Johnson 978-1-78952-236-5
Queen In The 1970s – James Griffiths 978-1-78952-265-5
Roxy Music In The 1970s – Dave Thompson 978-1-78952-180-1
Slade In The 1970s – Darren Johnson 978-1-78952-268-6
Status Quo In The 1980s – Greg Harper 978-1-78952-244-0
Tangerine Dream In The 1970s – Stephen Palmer 978-1-78952-161-0
The Sweet In The 1970s – Darren Johnson 978-1-78952-139-9
Uriah Heep In The 1970s – Steve Pilkington 978-1-78952-103-0
Van Der Graaf Generator In The 1970s – Steve Pilkington 978-1-78952-245-7
Rick Wakeman In The 1970s – Geoffrey Feakes 978-1-78952-264-8
Yes In The 1980s – Stephen Lambe With David Watkinson 978-1-78952-125-2

On Screen Series

Carry On… – Stephen Lambe 978-1-78952-004-0
David Cronenberg – Patrick Chapman 978-1-78952-071-2
Doctor Who: The David Tennant Years – Jamie Hailstone 978-1-78952-066-8
James Bond – Andrew Wild 978-1-78952-010-1
Monty Python – Steve Pilkington 978-1-78952-047-7
Seinfeld Seasons 1 To 5 – Stephen Lambe 978-1-78952-012-5

Other Books

1967: A Year In Psychedelic Rock 978-1-78952-155-9
1970: A Year In Rock – John Van Der Kiste 978-1-78952-147-4
1973: The Golden Year Of Progressive Rock 978-1-78952-165-8
Babysitting A Band On The Rocks – G.d. Praetorius 978-1-78952-106-1
Eric Clapton Sessions – Andrew Wild 978-1-78952-177-1
Derek Taylor: For Your Radioactive Children –
Andrew Darlington 978-1-78952-038-5
The Golden Road: The Recording History Of The Grateful Dead – John Kilbride 978-1-78952-156-6
Iggy And The Stooges On Stage 1967-1974 – Per Nilsen 978-1-78952-101-6
Jon Anderson And The Warriors – The Road To Yes –
David Watkinson 978-1-78952-059-0
Magic: The David Paton Story – David Paton 978-1-78952-266-2
Misty: The Music Of Johnny Mathis – Jakob Baekgaard 978-1-78952-247-1
Nu Metal: A Definitive Guide – Matt Karpe 978-1-78952-063-7
Tommy Bolin: In And Out Of Deep Purple – Laura Shenton 978-1-78952-070-5
Maximum Darkness – Deke Leonard 978-1-78952-048-4
The Twang Dynasty – Deke Leonard 978-1-78952-049-1

And Many More To Come!

Would you like to write for Sonicbond Publishing?

At Sonicbond Publishing we are always on the look-out for authors, particularly for our two main series:

On Track. Mixing fact with in depth analysis, the On Track series examines the work of a particular musical artist or group. All genres are considered from easy listening and jazz to 60s soul to 90s pop, via rock and metal.

On Screen. This series looks at the world of film and television. Subjects considered include directors, actors and writers, as well as entire television and film series. As with the On Track series, we balance fact with analysis.

While professional writing experience would, of course, be an advantage the most important qualification is to have real enthusiasm and knowledge of your subject. First-time authors are welcomed, but the ability to write well in English is essential.

Sonicbond Publishing has distribution throughout Europe and North America, and all books are also published in E-book form. Authors will be paid a royalty based on sales of their book.

Further details are available from www.sonicbondpublishing.co.uk. To contact us, complete the contact form there or
email info@sonicbondpublishing.co.uk